Praise for *The Insider's Guide to Online Fundraising*

"The Insider's Guide will be your go-to resource for how to launch, grow, and enhance your organization's online giving efforts from now into the future. Jen not only offers tactical tools, protocols and steps to effectively raise money and brand awareness for your cause, but she also addresses the importance of actively shifting an organization's culture to one that prioritizes investments in people and resources for digital fundraising success. This is one of those books that you'll be able to pick up anytime and learn something new to apply to your next campaign. I can't wait to get started!"

Katie Todd, MPA
Cary Academy Annual Fund Director
Former Director of Digital Strategies,
NC League of Conservation Voters
Former Board Chair, YNPN Triangle NC

"When it comes to success in online fundraising it requires equal parts creativity, execution, and passion for results. Jen provides all three in this book. Her stories will inspire you to create new programs and her tips and tricks will lead the way to help you find success! I ended up with pages of new ideas in my notebook. A must-read for anyone looking to bring a fire to your fundraising efforts."

Gregory Ng
Chief Strategy Officer and VP, Digital Engagement & Marketing
Former Host/Producer, Freezerburns

"Jen Newmeyer is a nonprofit change agent. Her digital smarts, fundraising savviness, and infectious creativity have had a lasting impact

on her station as well as her peers across public media. *The Insider's Guide* captures a transformational period of time when all staff realize they too are digital fundraisers. I encourage marketers, fundraisers, and digital teams who are eager to challenge the status quo to read this book and find strength in their efforts to persevere."

Chas Offutt
Senior Director, Development Services – Digital,
PBS: Public Broadcasting Service

"Jen removes the jargon and mystery of online, digital fundraising for nonprofits. Her book is an engaging read with relatable, real-world examples and actionable steps to improve online fundraising. She offers creative insights and focuses on all the right targets, such as the importance of knowing your audience, the power of words, and the often overlooked value of integrating with other marketing and communications strategies and tactics."

Ilina Ewen
Writer and Activist, dirtandnoise.com
Former Chief of Staff to the First Lady of NC
Contributing Writer to Walter Magazine

"I've been learning-and-doing in the nonprofit space since digital began, and *The Insider's Guide* is simply the best, most pragmatic and enjoyable book on fundraising that I've ever read. Jen takes us from simple ideas that a novice can put into practice to stepping stones for building a team and scaling up a comprehensive digital fundraising program. And she does it with the conversational, non-judgmental tone of a fireside chat. It leaves you feeling that any organization of any size and mission can do this — which they can!"

Alice Hendricks
CEO, Jackson River & Digital Capacity Builder

"*Jen is cooking with gas with her Insider's Guide to Online Fundraising! This must-have resource provides clear and colorful recipes for how to launch a successful digital fundraising campaign to build energized participation and new loyal donors. Real life examples with proven strategies and tactics can be incorporated into your organization immediately!*"

Amy Etheridge
Director of Development, Dorothea Dix Park Conservancy

"*Digital fundraising can seem like a daunting practice to implement in an organization. The Insider's Guide covers a lot of ground, breaking down the steps in a well laid out and organized way to make it seem more manageable. Jen's wit and charm shine through as she shares her experience and expertise.*"

Sandra Cyr
Managing Editor, Philanthropy Journal,
NCSU Institute for Nonprofits

"*Pull up a chair…because you now have the best seat in the house. If you are looking to make exciting and doable culture change and "shake it up" in your non-profit digital fundraising success, look no further than this book. It reads as an enlightening playbook for creating clear digital strategy and communications to get everyone working together, even those siloed skeptics, in a frequently misunderstood concept. "Someone is going to give us money, online?" Jen brings fresh energy to the ever-changing ecosystem of digital platforms and fundraising opportunities and helps the reader map out a plan for success for their digital initiatives and online efforts. You'll see how digital culture transformation is certainly on the menu.*"

Heather Burgiss
Senior Digital Producer/Director, North Carolina PBS, UNC-TV

"Jen's clear, direct and relatable style makes this an easy and worthwhile read. After reading the title, I knew my eyes would be opened to the simple truths to online fundraising. What I couldn't have anticipated is how expertly she untangled fundraising and workplace dynamics with humor while providing practical and applicable tools, techniques and strategies. This book should be as commonly used as a dictionary and on every community leader, nonprofit professional or board members desk."

Shana Overdorf
Fund Development and Program Strategist,
Certified Grant Writer, Community Advocate

"I just want a slow clap gif to be in place of actual text for my review in the digital version of this book! I worked alongside Jen for many years and bear witness to the hard lessons learned in the early days of digital fundraising. I found that I was holding my breath reading (and re-living) some of the tense meetings and close-call fundraising stories. I also found that I was able to fully exhale knowing that this knowledge will now be at the fingertips of others wanting to improve and grow digital engagement. It is truly an insider's guide. It is long overdue."

Christy L. Simmons
Communications and Marketing Professional,
C. Simmons Consulting

"With the accumulation of experience, data-driven focus, and persistence in organizations that are "digital-doubtful," Jen's incisive writing and deep experience provides readers with the whole gamut of everything needed to start or improve a digital marketing program. It includes campaign details and how-to, the mission-critical value of digital work, and a sense of fun that only someone passionate about their work (and results) can muster. I've always respected Jen's work *from a distance but this book sent my respect through the roof! It's a book I've needed and wanted, and will certainly help readers make a bigger difference in the communities they serve."*

Michelle Barber

Marketing Consultant to Nonprofits, Colleges, and Universities

Founder, Queer Coffee

Inaugural Digital Media Specialist at Vermont Foodbank

(2013-2016)

The Insider's
Guide To Online
Fundraising

THE INSIDER'S GUIDE TO ONLINE FUNDRAISING:

FINDING SUCCESS WHEN SURROUNDED BY SKEPTICS

JEN NEWMEYER

BOLD & BRIGHT
MEDIA

Published by Bold & Bright Media, LLC.
319 Becks Church Road
Lexington, North Carolina 27292
Boldandbrightmedia.com

ISBN-13: 978-0-578-56251-3

Library of Congress Control Number: 2019951984

Bold & Bright Media is a multimedia publishing company committed to bold hearts, bright minds, and storytellers whose experiences will inspire and compel others to grow in their own greatness. For more information visit BoldandBrightMedia.com.

Dedication

To Mom...

Your loving spirit lives in the song of the dove, the breeze through the trees, the bright sun in the garden, and in our hearts, forever.

Thank you for your constant support and encouragement, even when you needed it most.

This book is for you.

Contents

Foreword

I am delighted to write this foreword to "The Insiders Guide," not only because Jen Newmeyer has been a friend and colleague, but also because I lived the disappointment of tepid online fundraising results before hiring Jen and have experienced the delight and celebration of successive years of triple-digit results after hiring her. I want others to have that same experience.

Leading the advancement and integration of mission, strategy, and fundraising means that I believe deeply in reaching donors with messages and tools that activate them around values that matter to them. Our organization raises a significant portion of our annual operating expenses each year—most fundraisers can relate to that reality. Online fundraising is our most important tool in that effort. To illustrate just how valuable—in our organization, online fundraising has supplanted traditional public media on-air fundraising activity both in revenue and more significantly, in the much lower measure of the cost to raise a dollar.

Early on in my working relationship with Jen, after a successful online fundraising campaign, I wanted to reassure Jen that she did not have to follow a public media approach to online fundraising.

Her open, sunny and matter-of-fact response was "I adapt for audience and data but always follow the best practices for online fundraising and digital engagement. I apply those measures no matter the industry." After that first year of spectacular results, Jen went on to be tapped by our national industry leader, PBS, to lead webinars, to speak on national panels and to share her understanding and successes at growing online donor contributions. Yet, Jen Newmeyer has written a book for fundraisers and their leaders, no matter the industry.

In "The Insider's Guide," Jen takes us inside her thinking with a "recipe" for every imaginable fundraising opportunity: #GivingTuesday, peer-to-peer campaigns, special initiatives, end of year campaigns and other programs. She offers the tools and processes to make these results attainable for any organization. She shares her more than 15 years of fundraising expertise and offers encouragement and actionable steps to incorporate colleagues and other critical departments into the activities for successful online fundraising work.

The beauty of this book is the clarity it provides around a fluid, complex, sometimes confusing subject. The power of this book is its ability to help you produce your intended effects. While I've learned many great things from working with @CharityJen—I've learned many more actionable things from reading her book. You will too! As you read, you will want to share with others. This book can create a revolution in online fundraising by shining a bright light on how to do it well.

Susan Scott
Chief Advancement and Marketing Officer
UNC-TV Public Media North Carolina

Preface
Shaken Not Stirred

When I first arrived at the public media station in North Carolina, I was enchanted. At the end of a winding tree-lined drive, the studio was nestled amongst 100 acres of forest in the heart of Research Triangle Park. Deer would peek out from the trees, birds rustled in the bushes, and geese perched on the roof announcing the arrival of all who entered with loud and definitive honks. In the bright open lobby, large monitors proudly broadcasted all four of the statewide network channels. The studios were situated at the end of a very long hallway with natural light pouring in from the high second floor windows, enhancing the anticipation of arriving at the center of the network operations. Enormous, heavy bank-vault style doors revealed the magic of the massive dark spaces. The rolling cameras stood in powerful silence holding signs that reminded their subjects to smile. Zig-zagged across the high ceiling was a web of metal rails holding giant industrial lights ready at any moment to illuminate sets and stages. Immense black curtains that served as backdrops for the studio would sway slightly, mildly disturbed by the opening of the doors. Columns lined with buttons and knobs gave the feeling of giant mysterious control panels for the airwaves that extended 300 miles in each direction to the edges of the state.

I was fascinated by every aspect of this field, so different from the warehouse environment and scrappy nonprofit world in which I had worked previously. As I attended meetings and interacted with my colleagues, I felt like I was learning a new language: interstitials, lower-thirds, analog, OTT, bumpers, and microwaves (but not the kind in a breakroom).

One day an associate producer called me from an edit bay. "Edit bay?" I exclaimed, "what is that?! It sounds like something from Star Trek!" I ran downstairs immediately to see this small, dark, quiet room crowded with monitors and desktop equipment where the associate producer created marvelous programs. In the control room, I was mesmerized by the "mixers" and asked what would happen if I ran my hand over all the buttons like Buddy the Elf did in the elevator of the Empire State building. The director chuckled uncomfortably. "Um, yeah," he said slowly, "I wouldn't recommend that."

The first time I watched a live on-air fundraiser in the studio, I practically held my breath the entire time. I stood in the corner with eyes as wide as dinner plates. The countdown to the moment when the camera went live, the talent ad-libbing with no tele-prompters or scripts, the jump from one position to the next, the heightened levels of excitement and energy had me transfixed. Little did I know that less than a year later, I would be in front of the camera as a standing fixture for subsequent live fundraisers. Just two years later, I would be planning and producing them.

Despite my enthusiasm for this new environment, I had a job to do. Hired as the first digital fundraising manager for the station and most likely within public media overall, I was responsible for making money online. I already had nearly 10 years under my belt, building the online engagement and fundraising strategy for the largest food bank in the state. But as the weeks and months progressed, I realized that my new position was not only a challenge, but a proverbial uphill battle that would require every ounce of patience and creativity I could muster.

As foreign as the media world was to me, online fundraising was equally as foreign to my esteemed colleagues and others in the public media sector. After one of my presentations at an all-staff meeting about the new digital initiatives I was launching, one of the directors approached me afterwards and said in disbelief, "so you mean to tell me that you send an email and people are just going to give us money??" "Yes," I replied. "Yes, that is exactly what I'm telling you."

As I was soon to discover, digital fundraising in public media was a tough nut to crack. Stations rely on on-air fundraising as if lives depend on it. And who can blame them? For over 40 years, these efforts resulted in hundreds of millions of dollars to support educational, commercial-free programming. I began working with my teammates in other departments to break down silos and launch multi-channel campaigns that integrated mail, on-air, online and even social platforms. This not only enhanced the effectiveness of the on-air fundraisers, it boosted the performance of the other channels and presented cohesive, well-branded campaigns to our audience.

In addition to the heavy focus of on-air fundraising, the public television audience skews to older generations. Over 60% of the audience is over the age of 65. I discovered that digital efforts were met by some of our members with resistance and in some cases, downright hostility. So, we began online acquisition efforts to attract new and younger audiences as well as launching engagement campaigns that would be enticing to our older members. We began laying the foundations for consistent annual digital campaigns on which we could build.

Not only were we working to build integrated campaigns and focusing on the acquisition of a younger, middle-aged audience, we were also faced with viewers expecting a thank you gift for their donation. Analysis revealed that this kind of transactional giving was leading to members that were harder to retain and who were renewing their gifts at lower rates than a fresh acquisition audience who had never contributed to the station. Essentially, these donors are not giving to support the mission. They are giving to receive a DVD, a book or a tote bag. So, we began changing the language in our online fundraising communications to omit mention of thank you gifts or membership. We strictly used mission-focused themes, talked about the impact of these contributions in our communities, and incorporated testimonials from our existing members.

Internally, not all of these efforts were met with enthusiasm. Some of my colleagues were afraid of rocking the boat and were uncomfortable with shifting from language that had traditionally focused on membership with benefits, to language that asked for straight support of the mission. Many of them did not understand "digital fundraising" as a concept and confused it with social media or online marketing.

As I began attending public media conferences, webinars, and tracking discussions in online message boards, I was shocked to discover that these kinds of fundraising issues, and the resistance to new techniques, were pervasive throughout what is called the "system," aka, over 200 public media broadcast and public radio networks.

In conference sessions, new digital tactics were met with interrogation from the audience as to conversion rates, new member statistics, and renewal analysis. If a campaign didn't raise a certain dollar amount or result in a significant number of new members, the effort was dismissed. The concept of building a foundation for younger audiences on new platforms was completely obscure or outright ignored. In fact, in one session I presented with PBS on the results of a digital peer-to-peer pilot campaign, an older woman dramatically raised her hand and commented that she didn't understand this kind of effort, she would never participate in something like this, and she absolutely would not give a donation. This is exactly my point, I thought … you are not the target audience.

I was fortunate enough to have the support of the CEO and our executive team to test these waters with our viewers. I had a small, solid team that was willing and motivated to work together on new efforts. We were given the freedom to try new things and to get very creative with our campaigns. In the first year after my arrival, we grew online giving by 70% from $800,000 to over $1.3 million, without affecting the revenue of other fundraising efforts. (Caveat for those of you familiar with our organization: on-air fundraising did decrease by $600,000 but that was because of a separate, strategic effort to significantly scale back on-air drives and focus on net revenue.)

About two years later, we were asked to do a session on breaking down organizational silos and growing new digital revenue streams. The room was packed. Chairs were pulled up outside of doors and people were struggling to find spaces to sit on the floor.

After our presentation, which covered our restructuring efforts, the growth funnel we developed, and some examples of integrated campaigns, the questions that came afterward left me somber and quite concerned. It was clear that many people were struggling with how to get a handle on these kinds of concepts and implement them at their stations. It was a very real pain point for them.

Following this, I toyed with the idea of writing a book. I mentioned this to a friend of mine who works at a nonprofit focused on end-of-life care and grief support. She said, "Oh God, please do." She proceeded to tell me how her boss came to her just the week before and said, "I have a great idea! We should send some emails and ask for money!" She rolled her eyes dramatically as I nearly choked on my beer.

In fact, a 2019 Digital Outlook collaborative report published by Care 2, hjc, and NTEN examining trends in nonprofit organizations found that 35% still do not have staff members dedicated to digital strategy. Of the 65% that do, 10% of them are volunteers or interns. Clearly, many organizations are not embracing the tremendous opportunities available through online fundraising and investing in resources to implement digital plans and tactics.

Some of the information in this book may seem rudimentary to many development or marketing professionals, but I am addressing these topics based on real situations I've faced in my career, conversations I've had with other fundraisers, or discussions I've been a part of where these kinds of questions and frustrations have been expressed. The concepts I cover are related to scenarios in which there was a clear knowledge gap, where confusion was expressed in the digital fundraising and online engagement arena, or where situations revealed a lack of understanding from leadership.

Each chapter includes stories and anecdotes of my personal experiences followed by strategies, tactics, concepts, and plenty of ideas. Key takeaways for each chapter can be found in the Appendix for quick referral.

The book is divided into five sections: the basics, teams and planning, audiences and communities, campaigns and tactics, and the post-campaign activities. In the section and chapter headings you might also notice a unique theme. As a former "waitress in paradise," I have a heart-felt affinity for the restaurant industry, where I learned so much about working under pressure and developed a keen appreciation for dirty martinis to boot.

In Section 1, Prep Work, we'll discuss the basics of the digital landscape for nonprofits and public media. Chapter One, Building the Menu, starts with outlining the digital distribution channels and the distinct differences between digital content, digital marketing, digital fundraising and digital operations. We'll dig into how these categories support online engagement and fundraising activities. Chapter Two, Launch, will address the importance of digital and taking risks despite the anxiety and possible intimidation of online efforts. Chapter Three, Meat of the Matter, will break down the structure of digital campaigns and examines the techniques for crafting simple online efforts to robust, integrated initiatives.

In Section 2, Back of the House, we'll dig into setting up teams for success and proper project planning. Chapter Four, Shake It Up, will offer ideas for breaking down silos and encouraging collaboration between departments. Chapter Five, Ingredients for Project Success, will outline the tools needed to create an effective campaign strategy while Chapter Six, 86 the Turnover, identifies strategies to advocate for more resources to allow for growth and expansion.

In Section 3, Front of the House, we focus on audience and building communities. Chapter Seven, The Funnel Flow, examines the growth funnel along with the steps to attract new audiences and deepen relationships with donors. Chapter Eight, Special Seating, addresses the benefits of personalization and how to segment audiences into common categories for effective impact. Following that, Chapter Nine, The Regulars, discusses the steps to set up a successful ambassador's program.

Section 4, The Perfect Pour, takes a deep dive into digital campaign strategy and tactics. Chapters 10 and 11 (The Bar Nuts and Caviar) cover the roadmaps for successful engagement and revenue campaigns which includes defining the necessary campaign components along with a plethora of ideas and valuable tactics. Chapter 12, Happy Hour and Daily Specials, addresses the importance of prospecting for new donors as well as defining robust recapture efforts of lapsed contributors.

Section 5, The After Party, outlines post-campaign activities. Chapter 13, Closing Time, covers the metrics and analysis that should be performed to evaluate a campaign while Chapter 14, The Local Hangouts, suggests valuable networking and training opportunities available to aspiring and even established nonprofit fundraisers.

While the impetus for writing this book might have originated through my experiences in public media, it is not exclusively for those in this sector. It's for professionals who are new in their fundraising careers and need a solid roadmap for creating new online initiatives. It is for those well-established fundraisers who are ready to try something new or want to boost their existing digital efforts. I've written it for nonprofit executives who are leery of online efforts and for team members who simply don't understand the concept of digital fundraising but want to learn more about it. The strategies and suggestions apply for teams of one to teams of over 50.

My sincere hope is that this book will not stir things up. My hope is that it will shake them up. It's time to recognize the value of investing in digital engagement and fundraising efforts, and the benefits of cultivating younger audiences through online channels. It's time to work together, across departments, to create comprehensive, well-branded campaigns. It's time to toss the "we've never done that before so we're not going to" mentality out the window and begin to innovate, test, and implement change within our organizations. It's time to tackle the online landscape.

Let's begin.

SECTION 1
PREP WORK

Understanding the Basics

CHAPTER 1

Building the Menu
Defining Digital Channels and Categories

One of our major gift officers stood at my door with a bit of a sheepish look on his face. "So, Jen," he said, "I know you work hard here and your team is really busy, but what is it that you do exactly? ... What does digital engagement mean?"

A few months later, our interim General Manager, who came from one of the top news stations in the region, asked to have an introductory meeting with me. "Your department, digital engagement and fundraising, is not one with which I'm familiar. In fact, I've never heard of anything like this. What does your team do?"

Follow this up with a comment from one of our production directors who exclaimed in a heated moment, "Look: I gave my story to digital and they didn't do anything with it!"

Clearly, "digital" has maddeningly broad meaning. For some folks, the term digital could refer to clocks or cameras. For television broadcasters, digital represents the advancements from analog technology. For legacy IT developers, digital could mean binary code. When we start talking about digital engagement and digital fundraising, most people are scratching their heads in confusion.

At times, when I explain our efforts, people get a glazed over look as if I'm speaking another language. Just as I was immersed in the foreign language of the broadcast environment when I started working at our public media station, digital development work is equally unfamiliar. It's not only knowing the platforms and tactics but, more importantly, understanding the strategy behind these efforts that can be perplexing.

To really dig into the perception of digital from wider audience (as in, more than just my colleagues), I conducted a survey with members of local networking groups. I'll refer back to this survey throughout the chapter. The respondents included students, teachers, social workers, data scientists, and graphic designers. I asked them to share the first three words that came to mind when they thought of the word "digital." Of the participants, 30% of them thought of computers, 23% answered technology, 22% referred to the internet, while others indicated social media. The rest of the answers were mixed but included some shared responses such as coding, cell phones and websites. Other interesting feedback included paperless, graphics, and high-definition television.

It's not surprising that there is confusion when defining digital within our organizations. From the survey example above, no one equated "digital" with a nonprofit fundraising strategy. It is not a term that is commonly associated with fundraising efforts and can naturally lead to roadblocks if communication lines are not established and consistent.

At a recent nonprofit technology conference, leaders were debating the definition and organizational structure of the typical

IT department. The challenge is that IT is no longer defined in terms of the hardware needed so that an office can function properly. It's not even the support needed to make cables and connectors deliver power to computers and phones. As technology has evolved, the traditional IT department has expanded into software support, SQL server needs, security, managing devices, big data, and the cloud. The technology needed for an operations department is vastly different than the technology needed for marketing. For example, an operations department might require technical support for GPS-based activities and logistics, while the marketing department might need badge scanners and text communications for events. Defining and structuring the IT department can look very different from company to company.

Within non-profit organizations, we face the same struggles with the definition and structure of digital. Setting aside the broader associations of digital devices and technology, digital engagement and fundraising also has more than one meaning. It's a multi-layered approach to numerous online outreach efforts including digital content, digital marketing, digital fundraising, and digital operations. These functions can reside with one person or be assigned to various staff members in multiple departments. Understanding these areas is the first step in tackling the digital landscape for nonprofits and public media. It's building the menu for the tactics and strategies needed to connect with our online audiences!

Digital Content

Digital content is what we are producing for distribution online. It includes photos for Instagram, video for YouTube, updates of interesting activities on Facebook, news for Twitter, articles for blogs, and podcasts. Digital content provides people with helpful tips, breaking news, and travel advice. It ranges from cat memes to the history of bumper stickers. The information on our websites, the graphics used for digital advertising, and online publications such an annual reports or white papers all fall within the definition of digital content.

Referring back to our survey respondents, we found they had a pretty good handle on what digital content means to them. 32% agreed on social media as a digital content distribution platform and another 19% indicated that websites and blogs fall into this category. Not surprisingly, they also identified a wide variety of specific types of digital content including video, photos, newsletters, infographics, and articles.

Everything we consume online falls into the category of digital content. It is captivating, astonishing, and irresistible. Digital content piques our curiosity, and if done right, entices us to learn more.

In Chapter Seven, we will talk about growth funnels in which we guide our audience through a series of levels that deepen our relationship with them. Within digital fundraising and engagement, this starts with quality digital content. Digital content tells the story of our organizations. It is the first step in engaging with new audiences, it helps keep our supporters engaged, and it can provide valuable information to funders and partners.

Digital Marketing

Digital marketing is the intentional promotion of our content and activities. It includes advertising on websites, social media, or mobile devices. With digital marketing, we are boosting posts on Facebook, creating Google ads, sending promotional emails, and creating pre-roll video. This can involve subtle efforts—such as ensuring there is a donation button on the Facebook page—to more conspicuous efforts like home page pop-up boxes. Within digital marketing we are focused on search engine optimization (SEO) to ensure that our website has the right metadata and keywords, examining click-through rates to enhance emails, and looking at the number of likes and shares to help us tweak our strategy for optimum performance and reach. Digital marketing is not just advertising, it's also the laser-focused analysis of the data behind the scenes.

Our survey respondents also agreed on social media as a main platform for digital marketing with 47% identifying some sort of online or targeted advertising. Additional responses very much align with the concept outlined above and included webinars, cookies, data-driven efforts, and clicks. Some even associated the strategic goals of digital marketing such as "spreading mission" and "reaching customers."

In Chapter Five, we will discuss creating campaign toolkits and developing project plans. Within these stages, we are identifying the marketing outlets used for our engagement and fundraising initiatives. Once an idea has been developed with an objective and we create all of the "assets," aka digital content, how will we get the word out? Digital marketing covers this step, in addition to ensuring that these efforts reach the right audience at the right time to have the greatest impact.

Digital Fundraising

In digital fundraising, we utilize all of the content and marketing tools above to build campaigns that approach our audiences for monetary support through a series of touchpoints. Within digital fundraising, we use personalized messaging, optimized dona-tion forms, impact statements, and very clear call-to-actions (for example, "please donate!"). We might expand further to incorporate partnerships and sponsors for matching gifts and in-kind support. Email is a basic component of digital fundraising, in addition to a website presence, online advertising, and social media efforts.

Our survey participants were more familiar with the personal project and independent product funding campaigns rather than charitable online fundraising. 36% responded with crowdfunding tools such as GoFundMe or Kickstarter. Some of our survey participants were familiar with traditional digital fundraising and responded with associated phrases such as personalized email appeals, donate buttons, philanthropy, and connection.

While crowdsourcing can certainly be a part of a nonprofit fund-raising strategy, best practice involves building a consistent campaign calendar and a deliberate digital structure that aims to benefit the organization year over year in a more permanent manner.

GoFundMe is a platform for people to raise money for life events from celebrations or retirement to personal tragedies involving financial struggle, while Kickstarter is traditionally utilized for the funding of products or projects. For example, I had a friend use GoFundMe when his wife was diagnosed with a brain tumor and another used Kickstarter to help him release his first music album.

For charities, there are many crowdfunding tools such as Crowdrise, Causes and Indiegogo. But utilizing GoFundMe or Kickstarter for charity is tricky. Individuals can raise money to go to charity on GoFundMe or a charity can raise money for a specific creative project on Kickstarter. For example, several years ago, Reading Rainbow raised $5 million on Kickstarter to create a new learning app for tablets. For any organization considering crowdfunding, carefully examine the rules of the platform and evaluate any fees and charges that may be applied.

In Chapter 11, we will discuss creating effective revenue campaigns such as a year-end or holiday initiatives, telethons, and giving days such as Giving Tuesday. Other digital fundraising campaigns include walk-a-thons, peer-to-peer campaigns, or online auctions.

Digital Operations

Digital operations include the technical aspects of managing the platforms and production services of the three efforts above: content, marketing, and fundraising. This can involve building the components for a live-stream, handling on-demand video services, and working on the technical side of website management. It ensures that images are the right file size for faster load time, videos are encoded in the right file formats so they don't lag on browsers, and that html is written in such a way that it accommodates various browsers and devices. It can include developer activities such as managing and deploying apps or setting up APIs to work between an email platform and a donor database. Digital operations can involve building sophisticated online dashboards to view real-time analytics or creating workflows for email automation.

While a handful of the survey participants were unsure of how to define digital operations, most of the group had a pretty good concept of what it entails. 21% responded with the idea of some sort of management, either managing systems, infrastructure, files, or media. 11% associated digital operations with websites and another nine percent with social media. Other relevant feedback included online strategy and policies, development and coding, digital mechanics, and company operations.

Within a nonprofit organization, the responsibilities that fall within digital operations can reside in a number of departments. It is unlikely that one person is responsible for all of the digital operations, unless the organization is a small staff of one or two people (which is not uncommon, as explained in the next chapter). Within larger organizations, the production team might be responsible for handling live-streaming video, the IT department could oversee apps and APIs, the marketing team might be responsible for the coding of emails and the website, and the development or finance department could handle the CRM and data workflows.

The purpose of defining and highlighting digital operations, as fragmented as it might be within an organization, is to help colleagues understand that these very specific responsibilities could fall within several departments. We are aiming to point out that using the phrase "digital" is a generalization that could lead to a number of confusing conversations.

Categories in Action

Let's examine the above categories in a typical digital fundraising campaign.

Our hypothetical charity, Gardens of Good, aims to raise enough money to create a new community garden in their local town. They know how much it's going to cost and they've set a revenue goal. From there, they employ a number of digital tactics in the above categories:

- *Digital Content*: The team creates a logo and banners for a promotional webpage, they collect interesting photos of the proposed site, and they outline the benefits of local gardens for social media. A series of videos are produced to address the benefits of a community garden to the local residents. They write several blog posts on the impact of healthy food and include several fresh veggie recipes. A compelling white paper touting the success of gardens in other communities is published to the website.

- *Digital Marketing*: The news of the initiative is shared in promotional emails including all of the content above: photos, stories, recipes, and analysis. Facebook ads targeting members of the community are launched along with ads on Google, Twitter and Instagram. They post banner ads on the website spotlighting the campaign. The team engages a local news station to post digital ads on their website and they partner with a few local podcast shows to talk about the new initiative.

- *Digital Fundraising*: A series of fundraising emails are scheduled and point to a branded donation form. Local companies agree to match contributions to the campaign, which heightens the excitement of reaching the revenue goal. Marketing and digital content messages shift to focus on status updates of the goal. A series of testimonial videos from local neighbors are created to encourage gifts to the campaign.

- *Digital Operations*: This team is employed to create the responsive html for the emails and they ensure that the website is stable enough to handle the increased traffic. They monitor the performance of the online ads and help with collecting the data for analytics reports. They ensure contributions are processed securely and assist with any technical issues.

In addition to categorizing the above efforts, the remainder of this book will help with the strategies, tactics, and the best practices that are a part of planning and executing online campaigns.

* * *

While the general definitions for digital are vast and can be confused with the traditional concepts of digital in a wide variety of sectors, within engagement and fundraising, these efforts are specific, strategic, and measurable. We are utilizing online tools to move audiences through the levels of engagement (aka the growth funnel) by getting their attention, encouraging participation, engaging with them in a meaningful way, and encouraging them to become supporters of the mission. Separating the definitions of these digital efforts into content creation, marketing, fundraising, and operations will help colleagues better understand the intricacies involved with creating comprehensive campaigns and initiatives. It will define our departments and their areas of responsibility, it will help with communication related to promotional requests, and it will clearly outline the important work we do in this area.

> *Once you have mastered a technique,*
> *you barely have to look at a recipe again.*
> **—Julia Child**

CHAPTER 2

Launch
The Importance of Digital. And Taking Risks.

When I was about 10 years old, I attempted a backflip off the diving board of our neighbor's pool. I was adept at the much easier back-dive, but this was the first time I tried the added action of flipping all the way around. There were a couple of kids at this impromptu summer evening pool party that could do backflips and they had given me plenty of pointers. When I felt I had all the information I needed, I stood on the edge of the board facing away from the water. I took a few deep breaths, bounced a few times, and then launched. I went high enough but not out far enough. As a result, when I flipped over, the back of my head smacked the underside of the diving board.

I don't remember much of what happened next because I blacked out. When I came to, I was sitting underwater at the bottom of the pool. Fortunately, just a few seconds had passed, enough for onlookers to take a quick breath and wonder if a rescue was needed before I pushed back up through the water. Medics were not necessary, luckily, but I walked away with a nice big lump on the back of my head that lasted for several weeks afterward.

It's risky to attempt a backflip when you've mastered the form and flow of a back-dive. Moving to the next level can be intimidating, despite the number of people giving advice and instruction. But at some point, we've got to stand at the edge, take a few deep breaths, and launch.

I remember the very first email that I sent to an online audience back in 2008. It was a newsletter into which I'd put a significant amount of work. There were interesting stories, staff spotlights, and links to the latest press releases. It gave helpful tips of where people could donate in-kind gifts and the hours of our various locations. I was pleased with it. But more than gathering and developing the content, I remember the brief moment of panic before I hit the send button. Deep breath. Launch.

Luckily, nothing as dramatic as a potential drowning or a bump on the back of the head resulted from that email. While it may have caused some momentary anxiety on my part, recipients were receptive to the information and we proceeded to build on these digital communications to grow a dedicated audience and, simultaneously, a lucrative fundraising model.

Does that mean that everything moving forward was peachy-keen? Nope. There were times when technical problems caused systems to shut down during the height of a fundraiser, when goals went unmet, or overlooked typos caught the eyes of board members. Once we spent a significant amount of time creating a holiday honor campaign in which donors could send ecards to their honorees for a contribution. The campaign was immensely popular. People donated so that they could send 25 or 50 cards to friends and family. But the system wasn't working. We received calls from angry donors. As it turned out, the platform had a delivery block put in place to combat spam. Only 10 ecards could be sent within an hour. Therefore, a donor wanting to send 50 ecards had to log in every hour for five hours to send their cards. Certainly not a popular outcome. But these kinds of bumps and bruises are the learning experiences needed to build a successful fundraising strategy. Just as with other fundraising efforts, we learn as we go, making constant improvements along the way.

Even so, launching digital efforts can feel risky. The thought of them can prompt anxiety and momentary feelings of panic. A fear of failure can exist. Perhaps there is an apprehension of the unknown impact of digital information in the vast expanse of the "interwebs." People might find the technology intimidating. I've heard executives exclaim that their organizations are "very traditional" and there was no need to expand beyond their tried-and-true fundraising efforts, while others insist that "digital is only for millennials and we all know they don't have any money."

In actuality, the benefits of digital fundraising far outweigh the perceived risk. Online engagement allows us the flexibility to communicate in real-time, review results, and pivot immediately if needed. It is vital for diversifying a development portfolio and revenue structure. It's also the primary way to activate a younger audience.

Instant Results, Thrilling Campaigns

Online fundraising, unlike many traditional tactics, offers the ability to share results instantly. In the heat of a campaign, we can tally contributions up to the minute and build excitement with our donors as the thermometers climb while the clock is ticking. Updates can be posted to social media, incorporated in email, or even shared in a live video.

In one year-end campaign, we were in danger of not reaching our goal. There were only four hours left until midnight and we still had several thousand dollars to raise. In desperation, I launched a Hail Mary and reached out to our social media ambassadors to help us spread the word of our plight. Their impact worked! We met the goal with minutes to spare. (As an added bonus, all of this was done remotely from my couch at home!)

Of course, digital efforts may not always be related to revenue campaigns. These real time benefits apply to other kinds of exciting initiatives as well. Several years ago, one of our partners was intent on breaking a world record for the largest food drive in 24 hours. We spent several months planning and marketing so that when the day arrived, we had a captive audience. Food was coming in by the truckload and cars were lined up to drop off their donations. We posted updates, photos, and video on our digital channels throughout the day. Coming down to the last few hours of the drive, we were still far from the goal. The tension was palpable. Questions were coming in on social, text messages and calls to partners were flying, and volunteers were scrambling to reach out to their networks. Somehow, through a domino effect of communications, a message got through to the right person at one of our retail partners. At the giant food collection site, a tractor-trailer load full of donated food came rumbling in. Staff and volunteers scrambled to weigh it just before the 24-hour deadline. We met the goal and set the new world record. A veritable celebration was had on our social networks with our audience joining us virtually to share in the exhilaration and success.

In addition to the benefit of sharing results immediately, digital campaigns allow us to pivot quickly if our goals are not being met or audience feedback requires a quick change. In this way, we have the ability to fail fast and rebound even faster. If email number two of our six-part series has a shockingly large number of unsubscribes, we can make immediate changes to the schedule or the messaging and revamp the remaining campaign within hours. Our audiences might give us immediate feedback on social which allows us to alter the strategy of our engagement campaigns. If online ads are not performing to our expectations, we can pull them immediately and change tactics.

Direct mail, which can take months to plan and execute, does not give us that flexibility. If a campaign is floundering, we can't make any changes until the next campaign cycle. If a billboard ad results in negative feedback, it will take a few weeks to get those massive posters removed. If we made a mistake on a grant proposal, the odds of retraction are slim.

Digital campaigns allow us to pull back the curtain and offer a level of real-time, authentic transparency that supporters appreciate. The flexibility of making immediate changes can alter the outcome of our campaigns, allowing space for improvement and overall success.

Diversify With Digital

We hear it all the time from retirement experts: diversify your portfolio! They stress the importance of selecting a number of investments to weather the volatility of the markets and balance risk with success.

Within nonprofit fundraising structures, we must take the same approach. A well-rounded development office will have a combination of major gifts, grants, direct mail, corporate support, and events. For a public media station, on-air fundraising or membership will most likely be included. For certain sectors such as human services, in-kind donations of clothes, food, or other items such as furniture or appliances will be needed. Adding online fundraising is mandatory.

It's important to remember that adopting a new fundraising strategy does not mean abandoning others. As we've heard hundreds of times: a rising tide lifts all boats. This is true in the nonprofit sector as well. We aim to enhance, expand, and grow. Enhance the existing efforts with online exposure. Expand the existing audiences through engagement activities. Grow revenue with digital campaigns.

At the same time, diversification can be difficult for organizations with limited resources. In 2013, I gave a comprehensive presentation at an Association of Fundraising Professionals event that not only identified social media platforms and how they work but covered tactics, best practices, metrics, design, the use of hashtags, how to handle negative comments, the estimated value of likes and shares, and the importance of ambassadors, in addition to presenting three fundraising case studies. Obviously, it was entirely too much for one presentation. I'm fairly certain I obnoxiously exceeded my allotted time, but the organizers were too nice to interrupt me. Nevertheless, the first question I received was, "this is all great but I'm a staff of one ... where do I start?" The woman who asked is not alone.

I served on a board of directors for an organization that works closely with city, state, and federal officials to end and prevent homelessness. While the organization was responsible for handling hundreds of thousands of dollars in grant money to be dispersed within the local community, there was only one staff member. On a daily basis, her job consisted of preparing grants, writing grants, reviewing grant proposals, awarding grants, and budgeting for grants. In addition, she struggled to handle the day-to-day operations of the organization including corralling wayward board members like me.

In a 2017 report by Guidestar, 66% of charitable organizations nationwide are considered "grassroots," meaning they have less than a one million dollar operating budget. So, for these organizations, diversification is a challenge. It's important to look at the time needed to develop a robust program that will deliver the highest return on investment in the shortest period of time.

It can take up to two years to cultivate a major donor. It can take about three to five years to develop a robust direct mail program. Corporate support typically requires a marketing package with attractive deliverables. Creating a membership model not only requires benefits but also involves renewals and handling expired credit cards. A successful fundraising event or gala can take months to plan.

This is why digital is such an excellent option. A small organization can bring in a young volunteer or intern (trained and supervised, of course) to connect with audiences through social media, begin building a following, and work to develop an email list. A college marketing or communications major can assist with building basic emails to develop a small, impactful revenue campaign. A recent graduate with a little more experience can quickly place a few inexpensive online ads on Facebook or Google. In other words, the younger generations live and breathe these tools and are looking for ways to give back to their communities in the form of volunteerism. They are social media ambassadors waiting in the wings. They are a digitally savvy workforce that is eager to help. With a little structure and some branding guidelines, these folks can have an immediate and worthwhile impact.

For larger organizations who have the resources to invest in digital but are reluctant to dip their toe in the water, I will emphasize the importance of not only diversification, but also of keeping pace with the changing landscape of communications, audiences, and technology.

It is just as vital for nonprofits to adopt new strategies and innovations as it is in the corporate sector. We need only be reminded of the closures of Borders Books and Blockbuster. Some of us might recall with great reminiscence Radio Shack and Xerox. Who remembers Zenith or Studebaker? In fact, the American Enterprise Institute (AEI) reported a few years ago that 88% of the companies on the Fortune 500 list in 1955 no longer exist.

When we peek into the future by about 20 years or so, we will be marketing and fundraising to a millennial and Gen-Z audience. How will we reach them? The answer is: digitally.

Reaching the Young'ns

In diversifying a portfolio to add digital efforts to fundraising strategies, we also need to think in terms of diversifying *audiences*. On-air fundraising is successful with our older audiences in the 60+ year-old range. Major gift donors are typically in the 50+ category. Direct mail attracts donors in the 40+ range. The younger generations are online. They are on social media. They text and snap and finsta and watch hours of streaming video. We need to develop strong programs and platforms to focus on and begin to cultivate the "young'ns."

Charity: water is a ground-breaking nonprofit organization that utilizes digital-only tools for fundraising. They don't send direct mail. They don't communicate by mail. They don't print newsletters. All of their efforts are focused online, from member updates to compelling videos including GPS-based tracking of effectiveness of the wells in the villages that their donors help support. In the October 2018 issue of the Chronicle of Philanthropy, Scott Harrison, founder and CEO, was quoted as saying "we know that millennials don't give through the mail."

Scott was 30-years old when he started his organization in 2006. He knew nothing about charities or fundraising, but he knew how to promote his cause and he was passionate about providing clean water to people in developing countries. With this combined lack of knowledge and personal motivation, he created an organization that turned the traditional model of nonprofit operations and fundraising upside down. Major donors and corporate supporters cover all of the overhead and administration costs, which allows charity: water to apply 100% of contributor funds directly to projects and services. As reported in the article, they have raised over $320 million so far to solve the water crisis.

The model itself is a bit risky for traditional nonprofits. Two years after launching charity: water, the operating account was bankrupt with over $800,000 in the project account. However, the digital tactics they employ are a shining example of how a nonprofit can be successful in digital. They have a clear vision of their target audience and they understand intuitively how to reach them. The organization invests in high-quality video production to tell their stories, they utilize cutting edge website and email design, and they strive for brand excellence through beautifully produced content. For anyone still not convinced of the success of digital fundraising, digital marketing, and digital communications, they need only examine the tactics of this incredible organization.

Most nonprofit professionals understand the "churn" that occurs in various fundraising efforts, particularly direct mail. Donor interest starts to lag for various reasons. Individuals could have relocated to a new area, have had a change in lifestyle, or are simply motivated by something different. Even worse, perhaps the organization to which they contribute is a little lax on proper donor stewardship. Whatever the reason, just like feeding a fire, feeding a growth funnel is vital. This is true for our audiences as well. By simultaneously cultivating our older audience and launching initiatives that attract new and younger audiences, we are investing in the future success of our organizations. If we want to reach the "young'ns," we need to be online.

* * *

It's certainly understandable that launching new digital initiatives can be overwhelming and perhaps a little frightening. The quick pace of social, the speed of instant communication to hundreds of thousands of donors, and the technology itself can be daunting, not to mention the anxiety of making a mistake.

To illustrate, a few years ago I was texting my daughter. She asked why I was mad at her. I texted, "What do you mean? I'm not mad at you." She texted back, "yes, you are, you keep using all these periods." Apparently, proper sentence structure has no place in texting vernacular. (Confirmed in a Binghamton University study via the Washington Post that found that using a period when texting is received as insincere. Who knew?)

At some point though, we need to take a deep breath and fly off that diving board or risk being left behind, not to mention leaving a lot of money on the table that could easily ensure the existence of our organizations for years to come.

As for me and the backflip … I didn't give up. I just chose higher diving boards.

In any given moment we have two options:
to step forward into growth or to step back into safety.
—Abraham Maslow

CHAPTER 3

Meat of the Matter
Anatomy of Digital and Integrated Campaigns

A public media station had just completed a successful radio fundraising drive. The revenue numbers were stellar, guest engagement was positive, and the stories shared on-air were so inspirational that listeners and staff members alike were moved to tears. Overall, everyone was pleased.

But there were a few things missing from this seemingly successful campaign. There was little to no promotion on social media. The drive was not featured in any outgoing emails. There was nothing on the website that talked about the effort. The team was employing the same tactics used last year, and the year before, and most likely the same ones used 10 years ago.

In evaluating the overall initiative, there were a few additional pain points. The drive was 10 days long and staff members worked up to 12 hours a day. The schedule was relentless. Team members were exhausted. Listener complaints rose daily.

Taking a step back, let's consider several questions. How much more successful could a drive like this become if additional digital marketing tools were deployed? Could the drive end sooner? Could the hours of each day be reduced to more manageable levels? How many listeners cut off their radio when they heard yet another pitch for money on the fifth day, the sixth day, or the ninth day of tuning in?

Interestingly enough, these suggestions were brought to the management team of the station and they were immediately dismissed. After all, the drive was successful. Why mess with success?

As pointed out in the last chapter, the intimidation of launching digital efforts can stall the innovation of future fundraising efforts. Managers might write them off as a pesky request from the "newbies" or they might have a sense of aggravation for something else to do on top of everything else that has to be done. There might be a lack of understanding the importance of reaching a younger audience or the potential revenue benefit from crafting a robust integrated campaign. Perhaps there are internal silos that prevent the collaboration of such efforts.

To combat these objections, it's helpful to arm ourselves with information. Let's examine a few recent studies in which applying digital campaign tactics increased revenue and the number of gifts.

- NextAfter is a nonprofit research and consulting firm. In an evaluation of their benchmark clients, they found that adding email to an offline campaign increased giving by 90%. In addition, keeping email as a part of the future strategy increased retention by 29%. When crafting a robust integrated campaign utilizing multi-channel tactics, revenue was three times higher than offline only. Additionally, the retention rate of these donors was 56% higher. On another note, NextAfter has been performing these studies since

2006. Their first analysis of combining direct mail with email resulted in 60% more donations than direct mail. As we can see, these efforts have been utilized for over a decade.

- Dunham+Company provides fundraising and marketing services. Two of their clients launched integrated campaigns. One had messaging and brand alignment across all channels for a summer campaign. They saw a 68% increase in new donors over the previous year with a 10% increase in overall revenue. The other simply made sure the website and email had alignment with their mail campaign. This resulted in a 94% increase in total income and a 57% increase in new donors.

- PBS Development Services partnered with Carl Bloom to test the impact of social media support with an email campaign for 18 public media stations. They found a 25% increase in number of gifts and 40% increase in revenue when email is paired with Facebook ads.

While these results might help support the case of why an organization should start integrating digital and online efforts into existing offline campaigns, resistance might still exist due to a lack of understanding the tactics or an assumption that these efforts will be resource-intensive.

This is the beauty of digital initiatives. They can be crafted in a range of approaches from very basic campaign support to robust, integrated efforts. A campaign can be as simple as adding an email or a bit of social coverage to an existing offline initiative. It can be a stand-alone effort, separate from other fundraising initiatives. It can also be set up as a full-blown multi-channel campaign, utilizing all the tools from both offline and online efforts.

Let's get to the meat of the matter and examine the anatomy of a basic digital campaign, a more robust approach, and a comprehensive integrated campaign.

Basic Digital

A basic digital campaign can be utilized in a number of ways. It can be applied to a very short campaign that requires quick impact such as a one-day giving opportunity. It can be used for longer campaigns that need additional exposure over a period of weeks. A mix of the tactics can be used to support an offline fundraising effort.

Basic digital campaigns consist of emails to targeted or full audiences and social communications, whether these are social posts on Facebook or Instagram or paid ads on either Facebook, Instagram, or Twitter. The social posts are timed appropriately to support the email send or the timing of the offline effort. Tweets can be sent more frequently, as they are not under the scrutiny of algorithms. (Note: Twitter is extremely effective for advocacy groups or organizations that focus on timely news. Some nonprofits might not find the same impactful results. These campaigns can certainly be launched without incorporating Twitter posts.)

A basic digital campaign will typically launch with an email and paid social ad, followed by a supporting post on Facebook and/or Instagram. Several days later, another social post will reinforce the campaign. Depending on the length of the effort, a reminder email might be scheduled the following week with an additional post. Tweets can be scheduled throughout the duration of the campaign. The ads will also run throughout the duration.

Depending on the type of effort, the emails and social posts will point to a landing page that further explains the effort.

If this is a fundraising initiative, a webpage might provide a description of the campaign, the timing, goals, and a call-to-action. If it is an engagement campaign, the emails and posts might be directed to a form to enter a drawing, take an opinion poll, answer trivia questions, or view a video. Using the radio drive example from the beginning of the chapter, an online pledge form might be used.

In a one-day campaign, an email might be sent in the morning along with a social media ad, another email sent in the early evening, and a mix of Facebook and Instagram posts along with Twitter coverage throughout the day. A one-week campaign might have two emails, perhaps on a Monday and Thursday, ads will be placed on Monday, and social and twitter posts will be scattered throughout the week. A two-week campaign would be an extension of the above schedules.

	SUN	MON	TUE	WED	THU	FRI	SAT
WEEK-1			AM: Email #1 PM: Facebook or Instagram Post. Launch Paid Ad.	Twitter		Twitter	Facebook or Instagram Post
WEEK-2		Twitter	Twitter	AM: Email #2 PM: Facebook or Instagram Post	Twitter	Facebook or Instagram Post	Twitter (Paid Ad Ends)

Example of a basic digital two-week campaign schedule

Robust Digital

A robust digital campaign is utilized for initiatives that require more online exposure or are specifically targeted to online audiences. The robust campaign builds on the basic with email, social ads and social posts. In addition, it will incorporate elements such as external online advertising with partners, promotional video, blogs, Facebook live posts, Instagram stories, and/or an email series with conditional content, donation forms with dynamic ask strings, or website popups. A robust campaign might also include a company match with a heavy focus on meeting the revenue goal.

Branded assets play an important part in a robust digital campaign. Banners, ads, posts, and popups need to be replicated in the same color palette and design. The campaign name, tagline, talking points, and scripts for pre-recorded and live video require similar treatment. Across all channels, the campaign should appear coordinated in theme and messaging.

The campaign calendar timing is very important in a robust digital campaign to ensure that communication lines are not crossed and that assets are monitored across all channels with the proper messaging. For example, if the campaign strategy includes goal updates, the language will need to be updated across the board including any pre-recorded or live video, online advertising, blogs or landing pages as the campaign progresses. Additionally, the calendar will help the team stay organized and allow each post, ad, and email to have the highest impact.

	SUN	MON	TUE	WED	THU	FRI	SAT
WEEK-1			Launch. Deploy online ads, video and popups. AM: Email #1 PM: Facebook or Instagram Posts & Ad, Twitter	Twitter	Facebook or Instagram Post or Ad, Twitter		FB-IG Post, Twitter
WEEK-2	Twitter	Update Goal, Twitter	Facebook Live, Twitter	Blog Post	AM: Email #2 PM: Social Post/Ad, Twitter	FB-IG Post	Twitter
WEEK-3	Twitter	Update Goal, Twitter	Video Launch	AM: Email #3 PM: FB-IG Post/Ad, Twitter	Twitter	Twitter	FB-IG Post
WEEK-4	Twitter	Update Goal, Twitter	AM: Email #4 PM: FB-IG Post/Ad, Twitter	Twitter	Post Final Results to Website. AM: Results Email & Thank You PM: FB-IG Post/Ad, Twitter	Twitter Thank You	Twitter Thank You Ads End

Example of a four-week robust digital campaign for fundraising

Robust digital campaigns work well for year-end or fiscal year-end fundraising campaigns. We have used them for Nerd Trivia engagement and acquisition campaigns. They can be used for Valentine's Day honor campaigns, social fundraisers, or organizational milestones and anniversary celebrations.

Integrated Campaign

An integrated campaign is a robust effort on steroids. In addition to online campaign tactics, other fundraising channels such as direct mail, on-air, underwriting, and traditional marketing are employed. An integrated campaign typically makes sense when all channels are launched simultaneously such as end of year or end of fiscal year. The keys to successful integrated, multi-channel campaigns are to ensure assets are branded effectively, proper source coding is employed, and the timing of the efforts are mapped out to allow each of them to reach the right audience at the right time.

It is important to remember that these channels will have their own unique letter copy, scripts and posts that are platform-specific. The direct mail piece will not have hashtags. Emails will not be three pages long. Facebook posts will not sound like the on-air scripts. The integration comes from similar branding and phraseology that will revolve around a central theme. In one campaign, we utilized a Mister Rogers theme. The image of Fred Rogers worked perfectly in mail and on social but could not be used on-air during the drive due to competing programs. So, we used the term "Neighbor by Neighbor" with similar phrasing and color schemes that alluded to the concept of what the show represents but yet still tied into the overall campaign theme.

Integrated campaigns can be a tricky idea to propose to fellow colleagues, particularly in heavily siloed organizations. For example, when direct mail, on-air and online campaigns are running simultaneously, competition for marketing exposure can cause tension. I found great success in being fair yet flexible with rotational coverage. During a pledge drive, for example, the website features, emails, online advertising, and pre-roll video ads focus mainly on the drive. Outside of that window, direct mail and online giving share the exposure on marketing platforms. Each effort is coded appropriately and often requires individual donation forms or appending codes to URLs for proper tracking. The campaign schedule and deliverables are outlined in detail so that all departments are comfortable with the strategy.

Multiple calendars might be required to fully capture the activities of an integrated campaign. The example below illustrates the various overall marketing channels and the campaign focus for each week of the initiative. As mentioned above, direct mail and online giving share most of the marketing calendar except for weeks five and six when the on-air fundraising drive occurs. Shared marketing times and platforms might revolve around the "overall campaign" with generic campaign messages and a general call-to-action such as "visit our website for more information."

Let's examine a few of the platforms to fully grasp the concept of an integrated campaigns:

- In the promotional section of the weekly eGuide, weeks one and two will feature the direct mail branded ask and will point to the direct mail donation form. Weeks three and four will feature the online campaign and point to the online campaign donation form. The same goes for weeks five and six during the on-air fundraising drive. When the drive and direct mail windows conclude, weeks seven and eight go back to the online campaign.

- Pre-roll video promotion can rotate between ads, so weeks one through four will feature both the direct mail and online campaign until the on-air drive begins.
- The same approach is taken with Twitter in which multiple campaigns can be featured. When the drive begins in week four, promotion for all campaigns will be posted to the platform.
- Because the direct mail and online campaigns have similar messaging, radio ads will simply promote the overall fundraising time period and point to the website. Similarly, Google Ads will perform better with a generic call to action. On-air drive promotion on these platforms can revolve around program tune-in and more specific ads can be developed for those programs.

Weekly Rotation by Platform

	Monthly Member Magazine	Eguide	Email	Pre-Roll	Google Ads	Radio Ads	FB Ads	FB Posts	Twitter	Interstitials	Mail	Live-On-Air
WEEK-1	DM and OLG	DM	OLG	DM-OLG	OC	OC	OLG		DM-OLG	DM-OC	DM	
WEEK-2		DM	DM-OLG	DM-OLG	OC	OC	DM		DM-OLG		DM	
WEEK-3		OLG	OLG	DM-OLG	OC	OC	OLG		DM-OLG		DM	
WEEK-4		OLG	DM-OLG	DM-OLG	OAF	OAF	DM		DM-OLG-OAF		DM	
WEEK-5	OAF and OLG	OAF	OAF	OAF	OAF	OAF	OAF	OAF	DM-OLG-OAF	OAF	DM	OAF
WEEK-6		OAF	OAF	OAF	OAF	OAF	OAF	OAF	DM-OLG-OAF		DM	OAF
WEEK-7		OLG	OLG	OLG	OC	OC	OLG		DM-OLG	OC	DM	
WEEK-8		OLG	OLG	OLG	OC	OC	OLG		DM-OLG		DM	

A more tactical calendar identifies the actions taken during each week of an integrated campaign. The team can cross reference with the "weekly rotation by platform" calendar to know which effort will be featured.

Daily Campaign Action Calendar

	SUN	MON	TUE	WED	THU	FRI	SAT
WEEK-1		eGuide Launch. Deploy online ads, pre-roll and website popups.	DM Drop #1	AM: Email #1 PM: Facebook or Instagram Post/Ad, Twitter		Facebook or Instagram Post/Ad, Twitter	Twitter
WEEK-2	Twitter	eGuide Twitter	FB-IG Post/Ad Twitter		AM: Email #2 PM: Social Post/Ad, Twitter	Twitter	Twitter
WEEK-3		eGuide Twitter	FB-IG Post/Ad Twitter	DM eCompanion		AM: Email #3 PM: FB-IG Post/Ad, Twitter	
WEEK-4	Twitter	eGuide Twitter	DM Drop #2	AM: Email (OAF) PM: FB-IG Post/Ad Twitter			Twitter
WEEK-5		eGuide Twitter	FB-IG Post/Ad Twitter	Twitter	FB-IG Post/Ad Twitter	Twitter	
WEEK-6	Twitter	eGuide	DM Drop #3 Twitter	AM: Email (OAF)	AM: Email (OAF) PM: FB-IG Post/Ad, Twitter	FF-IG Post/Ad, Twitter	
WEEK-7		eGuide Twitter	FB-IG Post/Ad Twitter		AM: Email #3 PM: FB-IG Post/Ad, Twitter		Twitter
WEEK-8	Twitter	eGuide	Twitter	DM eCompanion	FB-IG Post/Ad, Twitter	AM: Email #4 PM: FB-IG Post/Ad, Twitter	Twitter

* * *

In essence, campaigns that meet their goals year after year will benefit from a little innovation and experimentation. What small tweaks in the form of basic digital support could ease a little stress from the team? What big changes in the form of a robust or integrated campaign could attract new audiences?

Simple campaigns are an easy way to dip the proverbial toe in the water by supporting an offline effort with an email or two and a few social posts. A clear and detailed calendar outlining the strategy for an integrated campaign will reflect the equal division of marketing channels during simultaneous initiatives. Organizing efforts in this way will ensure revenue attribution remains intact. It will also help obtain buy-in from different departments and divisions.

Digital campaigns help expand engagement, increase gifts, and grow revenue, in addition to the benefits pointed out in previous chapters such as fundraising diversification and cultivating younger audiences. But yet, some may view these efforts with hesitation and suspicion, despite years of research proving otherwise. Examining the anatomy of digital campaigns can help alleviate many concerns by providing a roadmap of the tactics.

The world is moving so fast these days that the man who says it can't be done is generally interrupted by someone doing it.
—Elbert Hubbard

SECTION 2
BACK OF THE HOUSE

Teams and Planning

C H A P T E R 4

Shake It Up
Navigating Org Charts, Silos and Lanes

It was my first day on the job and I was getting the standard on-site orientation: a swift tour of the main areas and breakrooms, a flurry of introductions to people whose names I'd forget just five minutes later, and a mountain of paperwork to review and complete within the coming weeks.

"Here is a copy of the org chart," the HR Assistant said cheerfully. She handed me a sheet of paper filled with the traditional rectangles and connectors. "Oh, this is great!" I replied while I quickly looked it over. "But where is the General Manager, I don't see his name here." She chuckled. "Well, this is just the development department," she said. She handed me another sheet for Marketing and Communications. "Here is MarComm and," she pulled out another sheet, "one for Content and another for Production Services, and oh, here is one for Technical Operations and, of course, Senior Management." She continued in her chipper manner as she pulled paper after paper out of her files like a magician pulling an absurd number of rabbits out of a hat. I took a deep breath as I fumbled with this new stack of materials and said "Oh, my."

Other than working for an international airline, which had nearly 2,000 employees in one of over 15 national reservation centers, most of the professional environments in which I have worked have been relatively small offices. The smallest was an office of two people: the Executive Director and me. The largest was about 85 employees but over half of them were in the operations department. So, in general, the development, marketing, events and finance teams consisted of about one or two people each. We had open access to each other quite literally because of our close proximity. I was in contact with our leadership on a daily basis. I could chat with my PR or Sales Managers over the cube walls. We didn't need to have water cooler discussions because we passed each other in the halls four or five times a day. When I had to meet with my team, we'd roll our chairs three feet away from our desks into the open walkways. In one office layout, the President could (and would often) bellow for me from his desk right around the corner.

Within this new environment, I learned that expansive org charts were very common at public media stations and, at times, even more intricate. Membership might be added to a mix of various structures within the development department. Social media could live in marketing, digital, or even IT. Marketing and communications might be separate departments. Graphic design could land in production operations or marketing. On-air fundraising could easily be in content or reside in development. How to coordinate a campaign within this somewhat chaotic environment?

As mentioned in the preface of this book, my boss and I recently gave a presentation at a national conference on breaking down silos within an organization and the success that comes from integrated fundraising strategies. The feedback we heard during and after the session was alarming. Membership does not work with social. Email efforts are not tied to development. Underwriting does not consult with marketing. On-air fundraising is stranded on a remote island (that may or may not have elaborate tiki drinks!).

In some cases, isolation such as this might result in "shadow marketing" in which departments start to assume the roles of their counterparts in the silo across the proverbial field. Flyers will be created simply out of desperation for promoting an event when they haven't been approved by marketing. Emails might be sent to certain segments of audiences because there isn't any coordination or ownership of a strategic email plan. Organizations could end up with four or more survey monkey accounts because no one has determined who owns these kinds of communications.

Additionally, these silos can result in staff members taking on additional tasks that are not a part of their normal job duties or that do not fall into the objectives of the department. Because the silos are so seemingly impenetrable, people might turn to their friends and ask favors. Managers might catch wind of their staff members building volunteer calendars, editing shows, or creating graphics for an event, all of which are completely outside of their job duties. Tensions between teams begin to rise and silos become even more solidified.

As the silos within organizations develop, departments tend to veer out of their lanes. Everything is looking fine from the outside but open a few doors or peek in a couple windows and there is mass chaos. It's like an absurd Abbott and Costello comedy show:

Who's on first?

That's right.

What's the guy's name?

No, What's on second.

I don't know!

He's on third.

Now who's playing third base?

No, Who's on first.

In general terms, silos can be helpful in defining the objectives of a department, but they can easily result in a frightening level of communication breakdown. This can not only damage the brand of an organization by making it look uncoordinated and sloppy, it will also make it nearly impossible to incorporate new digital fundraising efforts into the existing strategy.

While I've had my share of challenges launching campaigns due to personality conflicts or an unwillingness to participate, the lack of collaboration in many public media stations and nonprofits across the country is pervasive and causes severe frustration, in addition to the negative effects it has on the bottom line. Competition for revenue, the desire to be in the spotlight, aiming for professional gains; these can all be reasons why we pull our hair out, break our pencils in half and stomp home to guzzle bottles of wine because we just can't work with that team down the hall or on the other side of the building. I can't say that I can offer a silver bullet that will solve all the problems of breaking down silos, but there are a few approaches that might help.

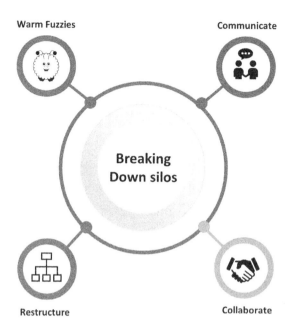

Listen.
And Communicate

Communication is a common recommendation for breaking down silos. However, the term is so broad that it's hard to know where to start. Most leaders might suggest staff presentations to keep departments informed. Perhaps an email from the General Manager or Executive Director to keep staff members focused on the mission might be helpful. Lunch-and-learns on particular topics might be offered to share with colleagues what new initiatives are being rolled out by various teams.

These are all fine suggestions and would certainly help with communication across the organization. But this won't necessarily solve the deep-seated tension between individuals and departments that prevent them working together on mission driven projects. Frustration among personalities might be so great that calls are not returned, emails go unread, or meeting invitations are declined. However, creating a safe, open space where dialog can happen could be the key to repairing these damaged relationships.

We had tension between two large departments of our organization. An executive coach with experience in teambuilding came to help us break down a number of silos that had existed for years. She began with a listening tour. Going to leaders, directors, managers and staff members, she worked to understand where problems existed. She held meetings in small groups to identify priorities, workflows, goals, and successes. What she discovered were a few very basic, solvable problems.

- Reporting structures: Individuals in other departments did not understand reporting structures which led to frustration when asking for help.
- Departmental goals and priorities: The strategic direction of teams was not clear to the rest of the organization and therefore led to a misunderstanding of prioritization.
- Projects in the pipeline: New projects were not shared widely which led to reactive implementation, haphazard communications, and a rushed promotion schedule.
- Needs and lack of resources: Colleagues were not aware of resource deficits in neighboring departments which led to assumptions of basic refusal of assistance.

A day-long meeting was scheduled between the two departments in which these areas were addressed. But the key to the success of this meeting was to involve everyone in the room. For sharing reporting structures, department leaders were asked to call their staff members up to the front one by one and introduce each of them. They stood in a cluster as each team took their turn until all attendees were out of their seats and on-stage. Department directors presented overall goals and priorities. Each manager was asked to share their individual projects, the needs of their departments, and recent successes. The highlight of the meeting was when the entire room broke out into small groups of six or seven people to discuss among their tables what they saw as major problems, identify areas that were working well and not-so well, and addressing resource needs. Each group recorded their discussions on slips of paper that were turned in to senior leadership.

Of course, not all of these issues are solved by holding one "kumbaya" type of meeting. But, it was a step in the right direction. Following this meeting, each attendee was assigned a "buddy" and required to meet once a week for 30 minutes for four weeks. Then buddies were switched. This one-on-one kind of environment opened the doors to honest conversations as team members began to understand the daily challenges faced by their peers. This level of understanding and empathy allowed for more collaboration and a willingness to help each other succeed.

Within our own rather large team with four distinct divisions, we took the advice of the tactics outlined in *Death by Meeting* by Patrick Lencioni. Senior leadership meets once a week for a "tactical" meeting in which each member quickly identifies three main priorities in their department for the week. The group votes on four or five of the most pressing items for the group and engages in a deep-dive discussion of those issues. Additionally, the entire team meets three times a week for a very short, 10-minute Work-in-Progress or WIP meeting in which everyone identifies their top three tasks for the day. This is a standing meeting: in other words, we are literally standing. It's a lightning-round approach to update team members. Any additional discussions happen afterward, informally. We also hold monthly strategic or "ad-hoc" meetings, as well as quarterly or bi-annual off-site retreats. These touchpoints ensure that everyone is on the same page and our overall projects and strategies are moving in the right direction.

Collaboration

Fostering collaboration builds on the first layer of listening and making space for open communication. But it takes quite a bit of patience and, in some cases, creative approaches to get groups to work together.

There are three tactics I typically use when crafting campaigns that involve multiple departments:

- Establishing a shared mission or goal to create a sense of direction for the group.
- Encouraging an idea-sharing environment that allows room for creativity and excitement to emerge. When individuals are given the opportunity to voice their opinions, they feel more closely aligned with the project outcome.
- Determining a project plan with timelines and expected outcomes that will set clear expectations for the group, ensuring accountability and ownership.

When planning and executing a 24-hour live-streaming digital telethon, I utilized not only internal representatives but also external social media ambassadors to help craft a unique and compelling event. The ambassadors were delighted to be a part of the planning process which encouraged an elevated level of dedication to the effort. Internal staff members were energized by their excitement which resulted in a shared desire to ensure its success and a willingness to go above and beyond to help with execution.

With on-air fundraising planning, we hold multiple group meetings in which a number of key individuals from each department participate. While I typically present a short introductory presentation with an overview of the recent developments, most of our time is spent going around the room, one-by-one, and allowing each member to ask questions of me or each other so that they can get clarification on plans, dates, times, and any other needs they may have.

In order to get the organization excited about Giving Tuesday, we offered a selfie station along with donuts and coffee for all staff. Following the event, we sent a recap of the day with links to all of the social media posts created by the staff members.

On long term projects or initiatives, brainstorming meetings might allow the group the freedom to be open and creative. Presenting metrics or incorporating benchmarks into meetings can show the effectiveness of various efforts. Creating a green-light committee could be just the thing when a plethora of projects, grants, or events are brought to the table. We've even offered lunch-and-learns with participatory activities such as how to create an Instagram story or tips and tricks for great selfies.

Overall, the idea is to create spaces where people feel empowered and involved while working together for a common goal.

Restructuring

Communication and collaboration are great in a healthy environment but sometimes the problems trickle down from the top. If leaders protect silos, then teams will protect silos.

Breaking down silos in an organization where leadership intentionally builds barriers to insulate their teams, protect their expense allocations, or even cover for incompetence can be difficult to rectify. Executive teams must closely examine the collaboration level of their organizations and may have to make some difficult decisions.

Our organization had a shift in leadership that allowed us to take a step back and ask some very hard questions about collaboration. While aligning our strategic goals and objectives, we developed a structure that would naturally encourage more innovation. We shifted workloads, moved team members into new departments, and dissolved old ones that didn't make sense. We created new divisions and hired leaders where we saw the greatest need. Ultimately, we ended up with a balanced department that supports collaboration, and communicates a clear vision and strategy.

How did we do it? We put development, marketing, communications and digital/social under one umbrella called "Advancement." Marcomm was established with two specific departments: creative services handling website, broadcast and digital graphics while the editorial arm handled traditional marketing, press releases, print graphics and publications. Development was split into three distinct segments: major and planned gifts, underwriting, and a new department focused on digital engagement and annual fundraising. In this department, we combined online giving, social media, annual giving, sustainers, audience services, and on-air fundraising with the goal of focusing on creating and launching integrated campaigns.

This new structure allowed for a more equitable distribution of responsibilities, giving leaders and teams the opportunity to become laser-focused on new initiatives to raise more revenue, increase engagement, and launch more targeted marketing and advertising efforts.

The Warm Fuzzies

The final recommendation to break down silos in an organization is what I call the "warm fuzzies." These are the fun activities that allow staff members to interact with each other in a personal, unstructured setting. They include social occasions, awards, team field trips, volunteer opportunities, or holiday parties. They can also include shadowing opportunities in which members of different teams or departments will join each other for a few hours or a full day.

At our organization, we have numerous awards that are presented at our year-end holiday party. Service Awards celebrate five, ten, fifteen and twenty-year employment milestones. The General Manager's Award recognizes overall outstanding achievement. Two additional awards are selected and voted on by peers. The Community Service Award honors an individual who participates in or implements community service projects either internally or externally. The Spirit Award celebrates an individual who exemplifies the values of the organization, consistently has a positive impact, and has the highest caliber of accomplishments.

For social occasions, we've scheduled Wine Down Wednesdays or Thirsty Thursdays at various locations in the area. A summer picnic or an outdoor hike offers opportunities for families and loved ones to join in the fun. We have yoga on Fridays and a lunchtime walk every Wednesday. A holiday party is how we wrap up (pun intended) the close of the year. As part of this event, we have an ugly sweater contest, table games, a slideshow of staff-compiled photos, and a dessert competition. The names of the annual award winners are mounted on plaques proudly displayed in the lobby.

A team field trip can include a tour of a local business, museums, or interesting attractions. Volunteer opportunities can include partnerships with local nonprofits such as food banks or housing organizations. Even a meeting with teambuilding activities is a fun way to interact with colleagues. One memorable activity we held was creating a "nest" for a fresh egg. Groups of four or five people were given newspaper, straws, duct tape, rubber bands and other assorted items to create a protective structure for the egg that was then dropped from a 25-foot studio ladder. Luckily, we had a set designer on our team, so our egg remained intact!

* * *

Change of any kind can feel disruptive. In a heavily-siloed organization, it can feel like an earthquake. When I started introducing digital campaigns at my organization, the shockwaves flew off the Richter scale. Some people were practically in a panic.

But to move forward, we had to shake it up. And it can be done. Breaking down silos takes time and persistence. Making space for open communication between departments, teams, and individual staff members is vital. It takes creativity to ensure engagement, and consistency to foster motivation. Creating opportunities for informal interactions will help strengthen relationships while building a culture of trust and support.

Leadership must promote and support collaboration, celebrate successes, and course-correct failures when needed. Executive teams should conduct regular evaluations of team structures and the organizational chart to monitor that the right people are in place to ensure that projects and initiatives are running smoothly.

Additionally, it might help to have a few rabbits and hats stored in the HR department!

We are all faced with a series of great opportunities brilliantly disguised as impossible situations.
—Charles R. Swindoll

CHAPTER 5

Ingredients for Project Success
A Canvas. A Toolkit. A Playbook.

"There was only ONE Facebook post for the event," she exclaimed dramatically, "only ONE!" She held up her index finger for emphasis as she glared at us from the end of the conference room table.

This was among a litany of complaints our corporate manager had for our team members during a post-mortem meeting from a major corporate volunteer event she had organized. Team leads, managers, directors, and even a few board members attended the meeting and the tension in the room was rising quickly.

The event itself was enormous. It took months of planning, countless meetings, an avalanche of emails, and required every resource the organization had to offer. All departments were involved from operations to marketing to finance. But even more problematic: the event was not well-orchestrated. Team members felt badgered into compliance. The expectations were unrealistically high. The ROI was painfully low. Not everyone was on board with the idea from the very beginning.

What became evident as we began peeling back the various layers of the proverbial post-mortem onion was that many of the communication issues experienced with the marketing and development departments could have been solved by outlining the deliverables to manage expectations. While our corporate manager was frustrated by the perception of a lack of digital coverage and recognition, had we explained the strategy on the various platforms, we could have avoided much of the conference room drama.

Unfortunately, situations such as this occur all the time. And, even worse, many great ideas for wonderful, fun, and engaging projects are tossed to the side from a lack of proper planning. Executive management might halt an initiative due to a loss of revenue when this could have easily been solved with a little extra push to find underwriters or incorporate digital support to raise additional dollars. A unique online engagement project might fall to the wayside because of a lack of resources when all that was needed was a group discussion to brainstorm creative possibilities such as utilizing interns or volunteers. A creative event might lose steam due to low attendance when the marketing or membership departments simply needed to be looped in to help with visibility to boost registrations.

What is needed to keep these ideas on the table and ensure the sanity of everyone involved is to properly outline the objectives, deliverables, resources, and cost analysis. There are three key ingredients needed for this approach: a project plan utilizing a business canvas, a campaign toolkit, and a comprehensive playbook.

A fully developed project plan utilizing a business model canvas template delivers the essential "vitamins and minerals" while including all of the necessary food groups. This is the main course!

A project plan will ensure that all departments, partners and clients are crystal clear on the deliverables. Everyone will understand their role. It will keep the team organized. Tasks will be completed in a timely manner. It will foster positive team collaboration. A project plan will outline the expected return-on-investment and the approach for developing future relationships with supporters.

Utilizing a campaign toolkit will help the team identify the basic components, marketing assets, and the strategic approaches available for the initiative. In discussing a detailed project plan, the toolkit will serve as the list of available ingredients from which to create a rich and fulfilling experience. All of the possibilities will be clearly identified in advance and will help the team stay focused on the objective, rather than veering off course to figure out how to add a component that is nearly impossible for the organization to deliver.

To round out these tasty dishes, a campaign or event playbook will serve as the scrumptious dessert. It's packed with all the delectable details of your effort. The playbook digs into the sweet granules that bring efforts full circle. From style guides to messaging to donation levels and premiums, the playbook is the resource used to document and track the details and activities needed to align the team, ensure proper communication, and make an initiative a successful one.

Project Plan

The goal of a project plan is to develop a clear strategy for an effective initiative. Through this process, team members have the opportunity to discuss and analyze various components of the plan to ensure that resources are used wisely, deliverables are achievable, timelines are realistic, messaging is cohesive, and budget expectations are understood and approved. A business model canvas is an excellent template used to meet the goals of each of these areas.

With a business model canvas, the following areas are identified:

- Key Partners: Who are the companies, businesses, board members, or others who will help with the initiative, whether through revenue support, in-kind gifts, or planning?
- Key Activities: What are the key activities? Is there an event component, a digital initiative, a marketing campaign, or volunteer activities?
- Key Resources: What marketing assets will be needed to support this initiative? What internal or external resources will be needed?
- Value Propositions: What is the benefit to the partners, supporters, and volunteers through this effort? What needs are we trying to meet or what problems are we trying to solve?
- Customer Relationships: How are we establishing the relationships with the participants, partners, donors, and or volunteers through this initiative? How do we maintain our connections with them?
- Channels: What platforms or programs need to be in place to reach our audiences? What is the outreach method? Do we need an online or mail component? Do we need event or meeting space?
- Customer Segments: Who is our target audience for this initiative? Is there a specific demographic we are trying to reach?
- Cost Structure: What are the expenses we anticipate will be incurred with this initiative?

- Revenue Streams: What strategies will be used to raise money through this initiative?

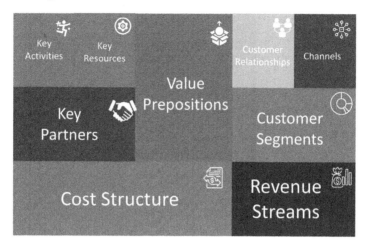

A Project Plan in Action

Let's outline a hypothetical project plan. Perhaps a local art museum aims to promote a new "Roaring Twenties" art exhibit. They hope to utilize this traveling show to boost museum visitors, gain new members, and raise the awareness of the museum in the local community. Using a business model canvas, the team outlines the following:

- Key Partners: Fashion and local lifestyle magazines. Champagne and liquor vendors. Jazz musicians.
- Key Activities: Kickoff event with jazz music, specialty cocktails, and a Great Gatsby-themed costume contest. Unique premiums and items will be available for purchase at the event. It will include a membership campaign. "Twenties Trivia" will be added as an acquisition and engagement effort.
- Key Resources: The internal event team will plan the event. The membership campaign will be managed by the

development team. The social and digital team will oversee the trivia components. This robust initiative will require a website landing page, registration pages, entry forms, organic and paid social, mail, online ads, photos, video, blogs, digital and print invitations, press release, flyers, posters, banners, giveaways, and event coverage.

- Value Proposition: Donations to the museum will support new shows and existing exhibits.
- Customer Relationships: Supporters will receive benefits such as exclusive tickets to future exhibits and discounts in the museum store.
- Channels: Website, email, and social platforms. Mail for invitation and membership updates. Event space.
- Customer Segments: Adults 25+ who value the arts and cultural activities.
- Cost Structure: The budget will address the expenses related to the event, cost of the mailings and invitations, pricing for the custom exhibit products, as well as the marketing dollars needed for print and advertising.
- Revenue Streams: Membership and sales from products produced for the exhibit.

Campaign Toolkits

Imagine a mechanics' workshop. Every tool is neatly arranged on a pegboard for quick and easy access. The mechanics understand the purpose and effectiveness of each tool. They know the outcome that each tool will produce and can apply them appropriately for the needed situation. When they give directives to associates, they can easily point to each tool and provide clear instructions. Their clients clearly understand the objectives and goals as they point out which tools will be used for the project. People trust in their skills and abilities because they understand the components and outcomes.

Identifying the "tools" for the support of a campaign is no different! Each resource is identified, defined, and matched with the objectives, goals, and target audiences of the project. Developing a campaign toolkit allows for project plans to be created with ease and encourages effective communication of the strategies with others in the organization. All parties involved understand the deliverables. There is no ambiguity.

To begin creating a campaign toolkit, identify the internal assets available for creating and promoting a campaign, event, or initiative. Work with colleagues in development, marketing, communications, social media, and perhaps even IT, to create a comprehensive list. Identify basic digital tools, marketing and promotional opportunities, and strategic components such as additional fundraising tactics or email content options.

A campaign toolkit might include the following:

Basic Tools	Digital Marketing	Traditional Marketing	Fundraising Tactics	Email Content
☐ Donation forms	☐ Google ads	☐ Press releases	☐ Matching partner	☐ CEO updates
☐ Registration Pages	☐ Social media ads	☐ Press conference	☐ Dynamic ask	☐ Volunteer or staff
☐ Survey/Entry forms	☐ Digital partner	☐ Editorials	string	spotlight
☐ Email	ads	☐ TV news/program	☐ Audience	☐ Client stories
Communication	☐ Website banners	appearances	segmentation	☐ Annual reports
☐ Organic social	☐ Blogs	☐ Radio or print ads	☐ Conditional	☐ White papers
media posts	☐ Preroll	☐ Flyers or posters	content	☐ Video promotion
☐ Website landing	☐ SEO and	☐ Banners	☐ Live-streaming	☐ Holiday or special
pages	metatags	☐ Events or meetups	☐ Donation overlays	celebrations
☐ Mail/Direct Mail	☐ Online video	☐ Print invitations	on video	☐ Recipes
☐ On-Air Component	☐ Digital	☐ Giveaways	☐ Lightbox	☐ Crafts
	invitations	☐ Premiums		☐ Event coverage
		☐ Ambassadors		☐ Photos
		☐ Board members		

Let's consider a few examples of utilizing a campaign toolkit that may not necessarily require a full project plan.

- Distribution of an annual report

  The organization decides there is no need to build a fundraising campaign or event around the distribution of an annual report, so the team decides to create a mailing to major donors, post a pdf to the website, and share the news on social media. At a later time, the annual report might serve as an addition to a more robust fundraising effort.

- Marketing for an event

  The event team is planning an informational meeting focused on new volunteer opportunities. There is no fundraising component, so the staff members decide on a website landing page, registration page, social media ads, digital email invitations, print invitations, a flyer, and banners.

- Basic digital campaign

  A local science museum is encouraging members to celebrate Astronomy Day. Since this is a stand-alone engagement piece, the team decides on email communication and social media posts. The links point to an existing educational video on the planets and galaxies, encourage the audience to visit a space exhibit at the museum, and include a donate link that points to an existing donation form.

Playbook

A playbook will answer a question that we contemplate all the time: "what happens if you get hit by a bus?" Rarely do we have the time to develop the whitepapers and documentation that outline in detail the workflows and training documents needed to easily transition to a new project manager or team lead. Typically, the operations of a nonprofit are like a speeding train, barreling down the tracks and focused on the day-to-day tasks to keep the organization moving forward.

However, in addition to documenting the aspects of a project for the sake of preparing for a disastrous situation involving a giant mechanical monolith, a playbook serves as a roadmap for holding a campaign year after year. Just as a coach documents play procedures to create team alignment and ensure effective communication, a campaign playbook provides team members with all the details needed to manage an initiative. It can be used to answer questions, keep the team on track, and record valuable details that are often overlooked such as hex color codes, scripts, and promotional calendars.

In a playbook that I created for one of our major events, I included the following:

- Overview, Goals, Target Audience
- Timeline
- Pitches, Scripts and Talking Points
- Donation Impact Statements
- Marketing Outline
- Flyers and Infographics
- Website Specs and Branding Details
- Event Kickoff: Incentives, checklist, staff assignments
- Post-Event Awards Celebration details
- Premiums and Swag
- Ambassadors, Partners, Main Contacts

A playbook can also include KPIs, budget outlines, or Gantt charts that outline the task deliverable dates. The playbook should include the project plan details or the business canvas model. It should also include a post-event overview that outlines successes, areas of improvement, and a financial report or event analysis for creating future budgets and goals.

* * *

There are times when coordinating large events, multi-channel campaigns, or major projects can result in elevated tension and frustration when teams are not aligned, communication breaks down, or there is a lack of clarity with goals and objectives. Taking a strategic approach to planning can go a long way in making these efforts a great success. A business model canvas takes a comprehensive approach to project planning, the campaign toolkit clearly identifies the tools available for marketing and promotion, and a playbook ensures that all of the details are documented for present and future projects. Carving out extra time to develop these three strategies are the key ingredients to campaign success.

Mix up a little more color here, put a little shadow right there. See how you can move things around? You have unlimited power on this canvas—you can literally, literally move mountains.

—Bob Ross

CHAPTER 6

86 the Turnover
Advocating for Resources

The organization was two months behind on the direct mail schedule equating to thousands of dollars in lost revenue. The financials for the prior month had not been closed and neither had the fiscal year-end. The auditors were scheduled to be in-house the following week. Acknowledgments had not been sent in over six weeks. There were piles of bundled donor contribution slips that had to be recorded in the database and a long list of voicemails from irate contributors that had to be returned.

Meanwhile, the development train kept running. Events were being planned, websites had to be updated, analysis for grant reports were due, and development officers needed reports for board meetings and major donors.

It was my first week at a human services organization and I walked into what could only be defined as pure chaos. The former database manager quit weeks before and took all of her knowledge with her. There was no succession planning for this role and the few training documents that had been created were several years old.

At one point, the finance director came into my cube with a stack of papers over a foot high. She said, "the month end numbers are off by about $140,000. So, we've got to go through each of these reports day by day, one by one." During team meetings, the Executive Director would burst in and say in a hyper-anxious sugary-sweet voice, "so, how are the numbers coming along? Are we caught up yet?" when we were still weeks behind. Since there were no instructions on the data export filters used for the direct mail campaigns, the first mailing we'd sent in two months was sent to everyone in the system. We discovered that the temp had been making data mistakes for weeks and all of her errors had to be identified and re-keyed. In the flurry of content approvals, we mistakenly mailed a card to tens of thousands of people that said, "food panties" instead of "food pantries." I literally felt that I had arrived in the seventh circle of hell. Every day, a new crop of problems arose.

But, as with all things, these issues were ironed out and solved over time. It took persistence. It took aggressive prioritization. It took a lot of deep breaths and an unrelenting calm demeanor. It also took resources.

In that first year, it was fairly easy for me to justify with my development director why we needed to hire a data-entry temp to keep the daily tasks on track. We were behind in so many areas it was adversely affecting the bottom line. When I needed to justify hiring the temp as a full-time staff member, there was a little more meat to the proposition. Two years later, I advocated to expand the department to add a second full-time data staff member to allow more time for me to focus on growing our online and social presence. A few years after that, I proposed to expand our digital fundraising efforts with a third full-time associate to take over social, our ambassador program, and launch a blog. Two years following, another staff member to manage the website and to help wrangle our increasingly complex digital campaigns.

Advocating for additional resources can be a time-consuming and challenging process. Often, nonprofit professionals will continue to plough through the work trying to do the best they can because it's seemingly easier for them to get things done rather than to train others. The thought of creating a comprehensive proposal for hiring additional staff members can be overwhelming.

This leads to a very common trend in nonprofit organizations: burn out. Nonprofit professionals end up leaving their organizations only to discover they ended up in the same exact mess they were in before, sometimes even worse. This is not only detrimental to the individual, but harmful to the future of the organization. It's tremendously disruptive to the operational workflow, it requires transitional training that slows any sort of progress, and, most importantly, leads to a loss of revenue.

Recent studies by the Society for Human Resource Management (SHRM) and the Center for American Progress (CAP) estimate that these losses can range in the tens of thousands of dollars a year, depending on the role. While some experts claim the cost is six to nine months of the salary range for a mid-level role, others predict the loss to be twice the annual salary for a director or executive officer. These estimates include the costs needed to advertise, interview, hire, and train, plus the time it takes for the new staff member to reach their full level of productivity.

As outlined in a 2016 study published by Nonprofit HR and Guidestar, the nonprofit sector contributes over $905 billion to the national economy. The growth has been tremendous over the past several years with a three percent increase in revenue every year. However, 84% of nonprofits do not have a retention strategy. Consequently, the organizations in the study reported a 19% turnover rate.

It's fairly common to turn to leadership and insist that they develop programs to retain employees. And certainly, there are practices that should be happening to help address high turn-over rates. But leadership cannot work to solve problems if they don't know what they are and if they don't understand where tensions exist. It's vital that employees feel comfortable speaking up about their workload. Complaining around the water cooler is not productive. It won't make the job easier. It will not solve any problems. Part of the ownership rests with the folks on the front lines doing the work. They need to be able to outline what is happening and offer suggestions for improvement to help "86 the Turnover."* If I had not taken the time to advocate for resources in my department, we would have never had the tremendous success we had in digital engagement and fundraising. I would still be sitting at a desk, ten years later, processing donations. Or, more likely, resigned to find a more interesting opportunity. (More on our success in Chapter 11.)

There are two types of approaches that can be used to develop a strong proposal to advocate for additional resources. A basic plan utilizes the "if this, then that" concept to present a high-level overview of improving efficiency, providing task consistency, and outlining the development of new projects. A complex plan is much more involved. It focuses on strategic growth and defines a three to five-year plan. It requires research, extensive data analysis, and budget projections.

Basic Plan

A basic or simple plan compares what currently happens against what could be done with more resources. As mentioned above, it is the "if this, then that" approach. For example, if we hire this person, then that will allow us to improve output by an additional 200 letters per month. If we get a new copier, then that will increase productivity by 40%. If we utilize the services of a volunteer committee, then that will allow us to expand our event by an additional 75 people.

When advocating to hire an additional person in our database department, my comparison was very straightforward. I outlined the current "state of the union" and weighed it against the impact of having another 40-hour per week staff member. Adding the additional staff member allowed for faster data processing and acknowledgements, in addition to an expansion of our website, email, and online advertising.

When petitioning for additional staff members using this type of basic plan, it's important to closely monitor the time it takes to complete tasks, so that a reasonable projection can be made for improving efficiency or outputs. In the example above, perhaps the new staff member would be assigned to work on data-entry for 60% of the time and acknowledgements for 40% of the time. This would lift the burden off the existing staff member, allowing them to segment website updates and emails using 30% of their time, focus on new program development and training for another

30%, and working on reporting and data cleanup for another 40%. Perhaps the plan might reflect an intermediate proposal to employ a half time staff member or temporary employee as a transitional phase. In this case, the focus on new program development or training might be reduced but would still allow for some of the basic needs of the department to receive incremental levels of improvement.

Me	Me + 1 STAFF MEMBER
• Data entry within 2 to 3 weeks • Acknowledgments sent every 3 weeks • Reporting limited • Website: Major Updates Only • Emails: Bi-monthly	• Data entry within 1 to 2 weeks • Acknowledgments sent every 2 weeks • Reporting monthly • Website: All Updates • Emails: 2x per month • Sustainer program development • Launch online advertising • Host team database training • Complete data cleanup projects

Elements of a Basic Plan to Advocate for Resources

If the plan is to advocate for equipment such as a new copier, the outline might include the costs associated with maintaining the current machinery (such as ongoing repairs) versus the savings of a new machine with an inexpensive maintenance plan. The proposal might include a comparison of the pages per minute or the savings on toner. Perhaps the plan would include an option to compare the pricing to employ a vendor to provide the printing services, taking into consideration the savings related to ordering stationery and staff time for managing mailings.

The purpose of a basic plan utilizing the "if this, then that" concept is to clearly present the benefits of investing in new resources while simultaneously outlining the potential consequences of doing business as usual. Leaders will be looking for improvements in productivity and workflow, reduction of costs, an increase in revenue, or overall impact. Addressing these questions and concerns when creating the plan will convey the strategic aspect of organizational growth to which they will be most receptive.

Complex Plan

A basic plan can serve as the building block for a more in-depth proposal or a complex plan. This type of plan will focus on strategic growth, examining the status of a department today and the possibilities three to five years into the future. It digs deep into what it will take to reach these goals.

Elements of a Complex Plan to Advocate for Resources

Identify Objectives

To begin creating this sort of plan, determine the overall objectives. What is the desired end result? How does this relate to the mission or the vision of the organization? Does it fall within the strategic priorities? Typically, areas of growth include revenue, donors, social followers, online engagement, or other mission-driven outputs. Perhaps there is a need to increase the amount of food distributed to those in need, the number of pet adoptions, or the expansion of educational events for a museum. There might be a deficit in the number of vehicles needed to provide statewide services or perhaps the expansion of a building is required. Once the objectives are in place, the research can begin for attaining these goals.

Gather Internal Data

Examining internal data will set the stage for developing the strategic plan. It will be important to have a thorough understanding of where the organization stands right now and what areas have the most growth potential. For example, our goal was to grow online giving. We took the annual online giving revenue and parsed them into categories, looking at the performance over several years. We discovered that, while sustainers accounted for nearly 25% of all contributions, the dollar amounts lagged far behind the other categories, ranking fifth overall. Additional reporting revealed that revenue from search engine traffic dominated all categories including campaigns and honor gifts. With this data in hand, it was clear that sustainers and online campaigns were two areas in which strategies could be crafted to contribute to the overall strategy, while building on the tactics for search engine optimization (SEO) would further improve the traffic to the website.

When aiming to grow areas such as donors, social engagement, or other outputs, look at past performance and evaluate particular areas of success or failure. What might have happened during those times that could either be optimized or improved? If there was a mailing that resonated with the audience and caused a spike in memberships, how can that initiative be replicated and tweaked for additional responses? What will it take to make that happen? Perhaps a social post was successful because of an endearing client story. What would be needed for the team to focus on collecting those personal stories for a blog? Maybe there was a time when acknowledgment letters were sent within the target time-frame of a week because of a surge of volunteer resources. How many additional hours were utilized during that time to make that happen? Could the team advocate for a consistent stream of help through the addition of a temporary employee? Consider applying a SWOT analysis (strengths, weaknesses, opportunities, threats) at this stage for help in identifying, clarifying, and establishing the goals.

Research External Data

The next step is examining external or national data to help create the case for the proposal. Are there growth rates for the sector that could play a part in projecting numbers? Have other nonprofits found success with a similar strategy that the team aims to implement? Perhaps there is a study that analyzed the increase of donor contributions related to the expediency of an acknowledgment letter or one that examines the benefits of a staff member versus a volunteer. Take some time to explore outside research to give additional endorsement of the ideas and suggestions in the plan.

When conducting research for my strategic 5-year plan advocating to expand the department by at least two staff members, I discovered an annual study in our sector that collected data on the number of development staff members in the organization as well as the annual fundraising revenue. When cross-referencing the reports and evaluating the value of each staff member related to the revenue, I was shocked to discover that over 60% of the organizations were in the range of attributing $500-700,000 raised by each individual per year. This data helped craft my onboarding proposal and projected revenue looking into the future.

Determine ROI and KPIs

The last piece to creating a well-rounded strategic proposal is to identify the return on investment (ROI) and the key performance indicators (KPIs). What will be the overall impact and how will it be measured? In my plan, this was a projection of growth in online revenue and social followers over the next five years with particular focus in three areas each. For online revenue: sustainers, campaigns, and contributions from online traffic. For social followers: growth on Facebook, Twitter, and website visitors. Within digital, other options could include email open rates or click-through percentages, increased participation in online engagement activities, or social expansion within certain online demographics. Additional areas might include increases in mail response, attendance at events with positive response rates, or an expansion of client services with the addition of space or vehicles.

As with a basic plan proposal, leaders will be most receptive to a proposal that identifies the problem or need and suggests a realistic solution backed with solid data analysis and supportive research. If a significant investment is required, the plan must include figures that address the return on that investment. Goals should model the SMART approach: specific, measurable, attainable, relevant, and timely. KPIs and benchmark reporting should be outlined with deliverable dates and a consistent follow-up schedule.

Know The Audience

The final piece of advice for presenting any kind of resource proposal is to understand the audience. Is the individual or group analytical and will they be looking for data-driven reports and comparisons? Are they creative and spontaneous, responding more to colorful graphs and imagery? Perhaps they are assertive and results-oriented, in which case the presentation might be brief and to the point.

If you're presenting to a formal board of directors, craft the presentation in a formal way. If your executive team is fresh and innovative, they might appreciate animated gifs to enhance your points. In a recent presentation that I attended, my colleagues knew that the boss was most interested in process improvement and so they made sure to include outlines of workflows. With a busy, creative team, perhaps add a bit of color but stick to the facts.

Leaders and board members have much to consider when making significant decisions on future resource investments. For large organizations, they may need to juggle multiple requests from various departments. For smaller organizations, it might simply come down to budget. These sorts of discussions can often be multi-layered and involve long-term strategic thinking. For example, when adding a new staff member, health benefits and retirement plans will play a major role in the decision-making process. If an equipment request, perhaps there are maintenance agreements or monthly fees that will be taken into consideration. Be prepared to answer follow-up questions and remain flexible and patient.

Ensure that the message is delivered in the most appropriate way with an understanding of the wider landscape. The audience will be more receptive to the proposal and willing to give it serious consideration. It displays a level of competency and elicits trust from the audience.

* * *

Taking the time to create a proposal to advocate for more resources will have benefits lasting far into the future. It will clearly identify departmental deficiencies, improve processes and outputs, allow for revenue growth, and expand the donor portfolio, not to mention reducing levels of stress and unmanageable workloads. Leaders can help staff members feel comfortable discussing these needs by encouraging the conversations and creating a safe space to do so.

With departments fully staffed and running smoothly, no one will ever have to worry about mailings seeking support for panties.

> *Yesterday is gone. Tomorrow has not yet come.*
> *We have only today. Let us begin.*
> **—Mother Theresa**

*In the restaurant business, when an item is no longer available, it's "86'd." The chef might say to the wait staff … "86 the chicken parmigiana," meaning don't sell any more of that dish, we're sold out. In relation to turnover, we aim to 86 it.

SECTION 3
FRONT OF
THE HOUSE

Audiences and Communities

CHAPTER 7

The Funnel Flow
Grow Your Audience. Deepen Relationships.

We sat at a long table in the center of a hushed co-working meeting space. Peppered among the cubes and couches around us were folks hyper-focused on the screens of their laptops eagerly typing away. We were surrounded by coffee cups and snacks, each of us with our own laptops ready to brainstorm and figure out the cornerstone of our future marketing, communications, and development efforts: The Growth Funnel.

At the time I didn't recognize how vital this awkward diagram would become to our future work and explaining our efforts to our peers. While certainly engaged in the discussion, I was simultaneously distracted by the hipster girl having a conference call at the high-top table along the wall and the wide variety of cookies in the vending machines next door.

Despite the curiosities of the co-working space, we became quite productive. We took the time to outline our collective work and plugged everything into each growth funnel category.

We debated some of the tools or efforts that spanned multiple categories. For example, couldn't Facebook ads be used for acquisition as well as cultivation? The website was certainly centered in the introduction phase, but it could also be plugged into the value exchange category, depending on the campaign or marketing effort. Did we agree that on-air fundraising spanned most of the beginning of the funnel while other online campaigns fell more to the middle? We nibbled away at chips and sipped cans of soda while carefully contemplating each activity.

Our growth funnel was to become the flagship of our advancement team. It guided the decisions we made with our campaigns and pushed us to think beyond a donation or a simple engagement effort. How could we advance the viewer, participant, volunteer, or donor to the next level? What was the next step in the journey? For example, at a kids or community event, could we capture email addresses by offering a drawing for a gift basket or t-shirts? If we had an online trivia initiative, could we encourage participants to share on social media or learn more about volunteering in the confirmation email? Could we do a Facebook live at a screening event and encourage participants to share it with their network?

The growth funnel helped explain our marketing and fundraising strategies to our leadership, colleagues, and even members of our own team. It helped them understand how every interaction plays a role in moving audiences from prospects to donors to advocates. While outlining and categorizing all of our marketing, communications, and development efforts was a tedious effort, and selecting snacks in the next room was often more tempting, the time we invested was an invaluable part of developing our goals and overall mission moving forward.

Growth Funnel Explained

From a visual perspective, the funnel can look like an inverted triangle or flipped sideways like a bullhorn or tipsy beer bottle. The concept being portrayed is that an organization is introducing themselves to a very large audience and, by moving the audience through various activities, the commitment of the individuals gets stronger and more involved until a mighty group of highly engaged advocates and donors has been developed. Not everyone will be interested or find alignment with the organization which is why the funnel visually gets smaller. We are focusing on a core group of individuals who find value in our mission and activities. It's our job to create those opportunities and experiences that encourage more involvement and, ultimately, volunteerism or contributions.

In sales, these efforts are often referred to as moving audiences from cold to warm to hot leads. (Some readers may relate to the phrase "Coffee is for closers!" from the classic movie, *Glengarry Glen Ross*.) But, as a fundraising organization, we are in the business of building relationships. Therefore, growth funnels for nonprofit organizations are a little more intricate and require much more grace and thoughtfulness.

There are numerous adjectives that are used to describe a growth funnel and the steps can differ quite a bit. For some organizations, there might be a few basic categories such as: capture, convert, nurture, and partner. These might also be described as exposure, influence, engagement, and action. I've seen organizations that simply delineate the introductory phase as "prepare and prospect" before beginning the donor cycle or the "moves management" program.

For the growth funnel at our organization, we settled on six phases:

- Introduction: Building awareness, helping people understand what we do
- Cultivation: Motivating an individual to join us, view our content, or learn more
- Acquisition: Compelling an action, encouraging a user to opt in or become a fan
- Value Exchange: Activating a donation or volunteer sign-up
- Stewardship: Deepening the relationship through recognition and acknowledgement
- Ambassadors/Advocates: Repeat engagement, a brand ambassador, or greater investment

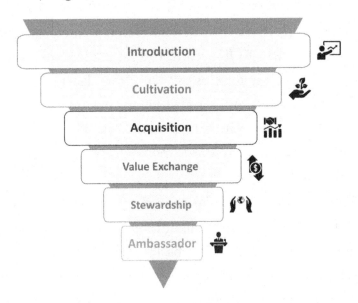

Growth Funnel Levels

Within these phases, we identified our target audiences. The introductory level would include anyone who we could potentially reach through any of our platforms, online or on-air. At the cultivation phase, we'd be working with our viewers or online followers. Acquisition would encompass our email list and could include the postal mailing list. At the value exchange level, we are communicating with our members. At stewardship, we're working with our sustainers. The advocate or ambassador level would include our major and planned giving donors, as well as anyone in our ambassador program.

We outlined some of the major activities for each level. As mentioned above, many activities will span numerous categories of the growth funnel. The website acts as an introduction for a new user and is also used for acquisition efforts. An event can act as a cultivation and acquisition effort or fall all the way into the stewardship category for members or major donors. Email is used in acquisition as well as value-exchange for fundraisers. Social media can be used in nearly every category.

Introduction	Cultivation	Acquisition	Value Exchange	Stewardship	Advocates
• Social Media	• Social Engagement	• Social Participation	• Social Fundraiser	• Social Video Thank	• Ambassador
• Posts	• Event Interactions	• Email Opt-Ins	• Event Donations	Yous	Program
• Events	• Ad Segments	• Photo Contests	• Volunteers	• Mailed TYs	• Board Participation
• Press releases	• Call Center	• On-Air Fundraisers	• eNewsletters	• Screenings	• Planned Giving or
• Marketing	• On-Air Spots	• Ticket/T-shirt	• Member Magazine	• Major Donor Visits	Estate Donors
• Materials	• Retargeting	Drawings	• Direct Mail	• Station Tours	• Sustainers
• Website	Campaigns		• Underwriting	• Sustainer	• Repeat Volunteers
• External Ads				Recapture	
• Blog Posts				• Member Benefits	
• Broadcast Programs					
• Podcasts					

Growth Funnel Activities

We also mapped out the various departments within our advancement team so that all members would understand where their work falls within the growth funnel. This fosters an environment of collaboration, helps during the development of strategic priorities and goals, and provides an understanding of how all departments fit together within the larger picture.

The Growth Funnel and Dating

In helping our staff and colleagues understand the purpose of the growth funnel, we compared it to dating. The levels of introduction, engagement, and stewardship are similar. It's all about deepening relationships and encouraging more active participation.

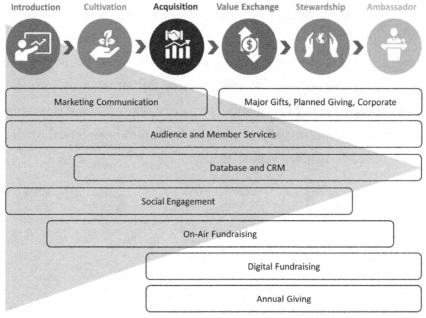

Growth Funnel Team Matrix

Introduction

Let's consider an individual embarking on the dating circuit. Starting from the very beginning, they might spend hours (or days or weeks) creating a compelling and interesting online profile. The details might include an overview of their interests, how they feel about certain topics, a few likes and dislikes, or some of their future plans. The same approach applies to an organization working from the start of their introduction to an audience: developing the mission, vision, values, and goals to clearly outline the purpose of their cause.

The individual might buy a new outfit for a networking event or a singles meetup. Perhaps they try a new lipstick or take a trip to the barber shop. This equates to the branding decisions of the organization. This dress-to-impress approach ensures that website, social channels, print materials, and advertising efforts have a cohesive look that reflects the personality of the organization.

Perhaps our hypothetical dating friend rehearses the answers to some common probing questions, "Where did you grow up? Where did you go to school? What do you do? Do you have siblings?" Essentially, they are creating a pitch and sharing their story. To correlate:

- Where you grew up = the origins of an organization
- Where you went to school = what makes this organization qualified to provide the services they do?
- What do you do? = tell me about the impact of your services in the community
- Siblings = who are your partners, board members, leadership, or key stakeholders?

Cultivation

Let's assume a connection has been made. The two individuals begin to talk more often and start to have deeper, more exploratory conversations. They discuss common interests and are surprised to learn that they both enjoy collecting vinyl records, exploring duct tape art, and speaking Klingon. Simultaneously, an organization is working to understand and pinpoint audience interests, likes, and dislikes. These conversations might be taking place at a live event or though incoming calls. Within digital cultivation, the evaluation of interests happens in other ways. What posts on social are receiving the highest click-through rates with the most likes and shares? Which ads have the highest performance? In this way, organizations can determine what is aligning with their audiences' personal interests.

Acquisition

Our two individuals are on the verge of taking the first step toward an official date. She might think, "Yes, he's rather nice, I like his haircut, and I can't believe he speaks Klingon." He might think, "Yah, she's kind of cute, I like that lipstick, and how cool is it that she digs vinyl." The individuals will decide if they want to exchange phone numbers. They agree to keep in touch. For an organization, the acquisition method might be obtaining an email or mailing address from the prospective donor.

The communication lines stay open as we move toward the value-exchange phase. At this point, we are more closely aligning interests as we work to deepen the relationship. Just like our dating couple will seek out the corner record shop, search for the next duct tape art exhibit, or book tickets to an upcoming Klingon convention, an organization begins to track interests based on conversations, email click rates, or participation in engagement efforts.

Perhaps it's discovered that audience members have passion for film and the organization provides thought-provoking documentaries. There might be a group of educators and the organization provides lesson plans and classroom materials. From there, a series of emails featuring documentary film festivals or the newest lesson plans might be created. Facebook ads related to these subjects would be targeted to the individuals. Perhaps postcards of the newest announcements related to these verticals would be mailed to them.

Value Exchange

The next level in our dating scenario and our growth funnel is asking for a commitment. The couple has enjoyed each other's company immensely and they want to make their relationship exclusive. They may decide on a boyfriend-girlfriend status, perhaps exchanging some sort of promise ring, or the big showstopper: marriage.

Lucky for us, the commitment for which we are asking is not so life-altering. In most cases, we're requesting a monetary contribution of any amount: big, small, or somewhere in between. What is most important in this "proposal" is that we explain, very clearly, the value exchange to our donors. These include statements such as:

- Your gift to our organization allows us to … [explain services provided]
- For a contribution of $35 or more we can … [outline specific programs this gift will support]
- Every dollar donated allows us to … [calculate direct impact for each amount]

Stewardship

The next step is stewardship! In the case of our happy couple, this would involve doing things like sending flowers, writing sweet notes to each other, offering to help with chores, or exchanging special gifts during the holidays. Stewardship at an organization may look similar.

Certainly, notes of gratitude will be sent, either in acknowledgment letters or special holiday notes. Perhaps a thank you video would be created, offering donors special theater tickets, or providing insider news like notes from the Executive Director. Additional activities might be outlined in a member benefits package which encourages giving at higher levels for more personalized and interesting benefits.

Advocates

Ultimately, we are aiming to turn our donors into advocates: life-long friends and partners. Imagine our couple years into the future with gray hair and wrinkles, holding hands as they meander through a park, happily chatting about the wonderful life they've had together. Their friends and family include a wide network of close relationships they've created over the years. This is also the goal of an organization. Turning donors into advocates helps expand the network. They become ambassadors, sharing the good work of the organization with their friends and family. From there, the new prospects are brought into the circle, starting again at the beginning of the funnel where we initiate the work of the growth model once more.

* * *

Thinking of a growth funnel in terms of building a relationship like the above dating example will help development officers and colleagues fully grasp the strategy of each level. This deeper understanding will assist with interactions that staff members have with prospects and donors, offering a more authentic and valuable experience.

Developing a robust growth funnel may take time and require the involvement of many team members. Depending on the strategies of the organization, the funnel may simply outline efforts at a high-level or may become quite detailed. It's important to determine where projects and tasks fall within the categories of the funnel so that there is a clear path for cultivating and growing the relationship with donors and volunteers. Setting aside the time to map these efforts will be time well spent.

Utilizing a growth funnel helps an organization and team members stay focused on the ultimate goal of creating a close network of advocates and ambassadors. It clarifies the strategy of fundraising and marketing efforts. It encourages creativity in identifying the next steps for audience growth. Donors will have a more gratifying experience as the growth funnel structure naturally aims to deepen relationships. It offers the ability for leadership to clearly understand the activities of the development and marketing teams, and may even open doors for additional support from board members and community leaders.

A growth funnel is an important component of developing an effective campaign strategy with clarity and intention that contributes to the overall success of an organization's mission and vision.

(P.S. Make sure you have really good snacks.)

Great things are done by a series of small things brought together.
—Vincent Van Gogh

CHAPTER 8

Special Seating

Defining Audiences through Segmentation and Personalization

It was a beautiful spring day. The sun was shining; the birds were singing. I headed to the mailbox and sorted through my pile of letters. Among them was an invitation to join an association for retirees. "What in the world is this?" I thought, simultaneously agitated and insulted. "Clearly they don't know me … I'm decades away from retiring." I tossed the letter in the trash, mumbling to myself about how that organization needs to get their act together.

It's one thing to be unknown. I think we're accustomed to receiving letters and emails addressed to the masses. Even the common "Dear Friend" salutation is typically overlooked from companies or people we don't know. Obviously, we're not friends with the CEO of the credit card company who conveniently encloses an application. Nor are we friends with the owner of the car dealership down the street who claims to have a special prize if we visit during their extravaganza on Saturday from 11:00 a.m to 2:00 p.m.

But it's an entirely different feeling to be "mis-known." Mistaken for someone or something else. Misinterpreted or misunderstood. For example, when a man named Kelly Smith receives letters addressed to Mrs. Smith. When someone spells your name wrong. When you are in your early forties and receive letters about retirement. And the absolute worst, when you're asked when the baby is due and you are not pregnant.

In general, I think we all want to feel like we are known in some way. We want our identities to be acknowledged. We crave a sense of belonging. To receive a letter that recognizes pieces of who we are gives us the sense of an established relationship. I feel more connected to an organization that states "Jen, we know you care about wildlife" more than one that says "Jen, we know you're faced with tough decisions about your assets." A. Yep, love nature. B. Nope, not on my radar.

It's like the Magic Mirror from Romper Room. At the end of the show, the host, looking through a giant magnifying glass, calls out the names of all the children she could "see." We'd wait with bated breath for our names to be called. "Romper stomper bomper boo… Tell me, tell me, tell me do … I see Gabe and Julie and Vincent and Rosalie and Freddie and Juan…" And when your name was called, you felt like the most special kid in the whole wide world.

While there is a sense of creepiness when we search for a computer bag on Google and receive a Facebook or Instagram ad for something similar only moments afterward, there is a bit of an interesting reassurance. Like, okay internet, you know what I like. You know me. I do like that fancy computer bag. And those cute sandals. And that Sagittarian t-shirt. Thanks for serving me more of what I want.

Personalization is a way to connect with one another. It shows how much you care. Imagine if Grandma sent us a printed letter instead of a handwritten note. Or, even worse, if she started the letter with "Dear Friend." We would obviously be concerned that Grandma was suffering from a severe case of dementia. (And shoutouts to my Grandma who sends pictures and holiday cash and regular updates about the pesky squirrels.)

The same principles apply to the segmentation and personalization that we use for defining audiences. Donors have made a personal connection with our organization by making a gift. One in which, for the most part, cannot even clearly be defined unless there is a chat over coffee to find out about the motivation for such support.

Unfortunately, unless we are major gift officers with a portfolio of donors with which to engage, we just don't have the time for breakfast meetings with contributors that can number in the tens of thousands. But we can give that same sense of "special seating" through a few common categories that reflect and recognize our audiences within the levels of their known relationship to us.

Donor Categories

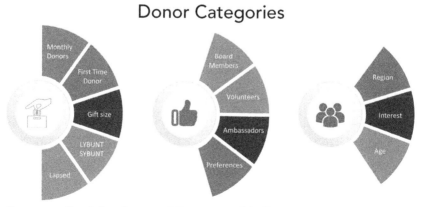

Revenue, Participation, and Demographic Segmentation Categories

In general, most nonprofit databases will record information that allows for segmentation based on several general categories. Organizations may be fortunate enough to have many more, but this will get the wheels turning. Let's examine revenue categories, participation, and demographics.

Revenue Categories

Monthly or sustaining donors: This is a golden group of donors! They are so aligned with the cause that they give month after month. Be sure to communicate the impact of their gift on a regular basis. Perhaps offer special tickets to events or a small token of appreciation such as a bumper sticker or pen.

First time donor: A new friend! Where's the confetti? Celebrate this new relationship by sending a special welcome letter or an email series.

Donors by gift size: Determine giving levels by calculating the number of gifts within pre-defined benchmarks. For example, the organization might establish a mid-level donor in the range of $250-$1,000, a leadership donor in the range of $1,000-5,000, and a major donor at $5,000 or more. Perhaps mid-level donors receive an annual report by mail, leadership donors receive an invitation to a fall gala, and major donors meet with a development officer once a year for coffee.

LYBUNTS and SYBUNTS: These are donors who gave "last year but unfortunately not this" year and who gave "some year but not this year." Many databases will have these canned reports built into the system but the parameters could be problematic. A donor may show up on a LYBUNT report that is run in June but they donate annually every October. Plus, you'd speak differently to a donor who gave two years ago compared to a donor who gave 12 years ago. Advice: don't use the canned reports but do consider the concept. Create custom filters that will look at these categories with more specificity.

Lapsed donors: Organizations may define lapsed donors a little differently, but the typical time frame is a donor who has not made a gift in the past 12-24 months.

Deep lapsed: Again, time frames are relative, but a deep lapsed donor might fall into a 24-36 month window.

Participation Categories

Board Members: The cream of the crop! People who care so much about the organization that they've invested time and energy to help lead it.

Volunteers and Ambassadors: These motivated individuals might fall into any of the categories above as well as serving the organization with their time and talent. Segmentation could be made within the volunteer file to further pinpoint their level of commitment. Example: Sustainer + Volunteer. Major gift donor + Board Member + Volunteer. Non-donor + Volunteer.

Communication preferences: In Chapter 12, we talk about the opportunity to engage audiences based on their communication preferences. For example, folks who have opted out of email can be targeted for Facebook ads.

Demographic Categories

Region: Hometown pride is a thing! Consider segmenting audiences based on the county in which they reside.

Interests: It can be a challenge to determine your audience interests but gathering data along the way can help make the process easier. Consider tagging accounts from email signups based on certain categories, entries for drawings, event signups, or by conducting old-fashioned surveys.

Age: As with interests, it can be difficult to capture birth dates, but these are wonderful opportunities for targeted communications. The most obvious would be a birthday greeting with a special video message from the Executive Director or staff. Looking at ages can inform campaigns such as planned giving opportunities or bequests. Knowing the age range of donors at various giving levels can help with more appropriate language in direct communications.

Segmentation Strategies & Examples

Segmentation does not have to be a complex or involved task. Some very simple language shifted in a campaign email can do the trick. Utilizing "conditional" tags or content can easily personalize a message to various groups.

Let's examine a year-end email appeal to a few very basic donor groups for a hypothetical charity providing emotional support through equine therapy. In this example, we are adjusting language for a sustainer, a recent one-time donor, a lapsed donor, and a non-donor. In the sustainer letter, we overemphasize gratitude and simply ask them to share the campaign. For a one-time donor, we offer gratitude but highlight the impact of the work and ask for an additional gift. With the lapsed donor, we focus on a direct ask. For a non-donor, we educate as well as asking for a gift.

Dear Mary,

Celia is a five-year old who came to Sunnyside Center two years ago when her parents started having trouble at home. After Dad lost his job and Mom became ill, Celia found

94

support through these tough times by forming a bond with Harvey, one of Sunnyside's longest resident rescue horses. Celia and Harvey could be found on long rides through the Sunnyside fields. "Spending time with Harvey allowed me to relax and enjoy the outdoors while my parents worked through a lot of family problems."

[Conditional language to sustainers]

As you know, Sunnyside Center of Apple County supports children and their families through equine-assisted therapy. We provide classes and workshops for at-risk children with the goal of improving mental health.

As a monthly donor, we thank you for your ongoing support. Your consistent gifts ensure that we have the resources to continue our important work. We are holding a Holiday Campaign and aim to raise $50,000 before December 31. As a valued sustainer, would you please share the campaign with your friends and family and encourage them to join you as a valued contributor?

[Conditional language to a one-time donor in the past year, excluding sustainers and recent donors in the past four to six weeks]

As you know, Sunnyside Center of Apple County supports children and their families through equine-assisted therapy. We provide classes and workshops for at-risk children with the goal of improving mental health.

We'd like to thank you again for your contribution this past year. Your gift ensures that we have the resources to support our important work, and that work continues. We are holding a Holiday Campaign and aim to raise $50,000 before December 31. This campaign is vital to providing services to children just like Celia. Would you consider making a second gift to support this important campaign?

[Conditional language to lapsed donor]

As you know, Sunnyside Center of Apple County supports children and their families through equine-assisted therapy. We provide classes and workshops for at-risk children with the goal of improving mental health.

We are holding a Holiday Campaign and aim to raise $50,000 before December 31. Would you consider renewing your support through this important campaign? Your gift means so much to children just like Celia. Every dollar counts!

[Conditional language to non-donors or prospects]

Sunnyside Center of Apple County supports children and their families through equine-assisted therapy. Established in 2014, we have 28 acres of rolling pastures for our nine rescue horses. Through our 27,000 square-foot center, barn and riding arena, we provide classes and workshops for at-risk children with the goal of improving mental health. Over 300 children have received assistance from our organization.

We are holding a Holiday Campaign and aim to raise $50,000 before December 31. Would you consider supporting this important campaign? Your gift means so much to children just like Celia. Every dollar counts!

Similar approaches can be used for other outreach. Consider invitations to a gala. Segmentation and taglines might look like this:

Attended Gala last year

> *We were so happy to see you last year at the Apple Gala. Join us again for a fabulous time!*

Attended Gala previous year but not last year

> *We missed you last year but hope you will be able to join us again.*

Never attended Gala, but has been involved with the organization recently (donation, volunteer, other event attendee)

> *This is an excellent opportunity to not only show your support for the organization but also to interact with a dynamic group of people who share the same interest in equine-assisted therapy!*

Prospects

> *Have you heard of the Apple Gala to support Sunnyside Center? It's our annual event to raise $75,000 for children and their families through equine-assisted therapy. Please join us!*

More direct language can be used in Facebook ads. Consider these ideas for a trivia engagement campaign to the following groups:

Donors and volunteers within Apple County

> *You know Apply County. You love Apple County. Test your Apple County Horse History knowledge through the Sunnyside Center March Trivia Challenge!*

Donors and volunteers outside of Apple County

> *How much do you know about Apple County Horse History? Test your knowledge today through the Sunnyside Center March Trivia Challenge!*

Non-donors (such as email lists) or prospects

> *The horses of Apple County are calling! How much do you know about their history? Test your knowledge today through the Sunnyside Center March Trivia Challenge!*

Data Hygiene

Segmentation efforts will be worthless if the database is not clean, so keep data hygiene practices at the top of the priority list. In addition to ensuring that donor accounts are properly recorded, these efforts will produce reliable reports and save the organization money that would otherwise be wasted on duplicate or incorrect mailings. There are several common ways to ensure that the system is in good shape.

Standard Practices: As the saying goes: bad data in, bad data out. Ensure that data-entry practices are outlined in a clear and thorough way. Before entering a new account, what are the policies for searching the system for an existing account? For example, the steps might include searching on the last name, searching a portion of the last name and a portion of the address, or searching on the last name and city. When similar accounts are found, what is the policy for changing addresses? Perhaps the steps involve verifying the date of the last change to the account before adding a new address. There might also be guidelines for merging accounts, linking related accounts, and requiring notes for any changes made to accounts.

Duplicate Checks: On a quarterly or bi-monthly basis, the database should be scanned for duplicates so that accounts can be merged and updated. While this is often a tedious process, it could save the organization hundreds of dollars on wasted mailings, not to mention the embarrassment of donors receiving multiple mailings.

Requested Updates: Of course, requests for changes to accounts should be handled promptly. If a donor or volunteer makes the effort to contact the organization with a change, they are displaying the dedication and investment they have in the relationship. The same respect should be shown by honoring their request swiftly.

Outside Resources: If the organization utilizes the services of a direct mail vendor, a NCOA (National Change of Address) scan will be performed on the mailing list. These updates should be regularly loaded into the system. Data screenings for age, wealth, or interests will be valuable for gathering additional information about donors.

* * *

Speaking to our donors through personalization by utilizing segmentation allows us to connect with them in a sincere and authentic way. It acknowledges their relationship with the organization and reflects the value of the partnership. It elicits a sense of trust and reassurance. And, as long as our data is correct, it shows that the organization is proficient and responsible.

Just like walking into a restaurant where everybody knows your name, we can create that same sense of connection and belonging with our valued supporters by recognizing them in these small but impactful ways.

The world needs a sense of worth, and it will achieve it
only by its people feeling that they are worthwhile.
—Fred Rogers

CHAPTER 9

The Regulars

The Power of an Ambassador Program

"I want to do something really big for the organization," he explained, "something powerful and different." We were crowded around a phone listening patiently as Greg shared his ideas with excitement. He was one of our newest social media ambassadors and was ready to dive in to a new project. "I've done a lot of live-streaming events and I think I can make a big impact for you," he said.

At the time, we were approached on a weekly, if not a daily basis by people wanting to partner with us on community projects. Our mission resonated with folks and they were motivated to help. But our staffing resources were extremely limited, and we had to be judicious with our time. So, I listened to Greg with a slightly guarded disposition as he went on to share his ideas.

"I'd be live for a full 24-hours online. We'd get partners to donate. I'd interview them. We could do it from your warehouse, maybe talk to staff members or volunteers. We'd really show the impact of how you help children and families," he said. I took a deep breath. A 24-hour event? When we were struggling to keep up with the events we already had? It was a tall order. I was skeptical.

But then Greg said, "I have an online show and have been doing a weekly episode for about six years. I'd tap into that network. There are over 600,000 subscribers." We gasped and stared at each other. 600,000? Six. Hundred. Thousand?? My heart skipped a beat. I took another deep breath, but this time to restrain my urge to jump for joy. "Greg," I said with as much calm in my voice as I could muster, "why don't you let me bring some more folks into the conversation. Let's arrange a time for you to come over for a face-to-face meeting."

We made our plans and hung up the phone. Then we screamed. And jumped for joy.

Following this call, we utilized Greg's network, our ambassadors and partners, staff members and their family and friends, our volunteers, and even our warehouse neighbors to launch a 24-hour live-streaming Telethon that raised over $50,000 year after year for nearly five straight years. The show consisted of back-to-back partner and volunteer interviews, celebrity appearances, blindfold tasting challenges, cake decorating competitions, and check presentations. We interjected events where the general public could join us for tours, games, prizes and snacks. We brought in a dunk tank to encourage donations during certain time frames. We dunked our CEO! We offered volunteering opportunities, dance lessons, food trucks, and even had sunrise yoga with our peas and carrots mascots. It was a unique fundraising event that combined community outreach and partner involvement both online and in-person.

Ambassadors are power-house volunteers. They are the superstars of an organization. They increase the awareness of the mission and propel community impact by utilizing their personal and professional networks. They help extend and boost the marketing of an organization. In addition, they help drive action for campaigns, whether attracting new prospects or increasing revenue. Why? Because they are trusted.

In a comprehensive study by Nielsen of over 30,000 people in 60 countries, 83% of participants indicated that they trust the recommendations of friends and family when it comes to products and services. In comparison, trust in traditional advertising such as magazines or newspapers ranged from 50-52% while trust in online ads ranged from 33-38%.

When someone hears a friend or family member talking about a book, a restaurant, a brand of clothing, or even the friendly cashier at the local hardware store, people are more likely to investigate those things than they are by seeing a billboard or TV ad. Encouraging supporters to become ambassadors helps expand the network of an organization in an authentic way.

But the impact of ambassadors is not only limited to friends and family. In 2012, a small group of Nikola Tesla fans were desperately trying to figure out how to purchase a $1.6 million tract of land in New York that had previously been owned by the famous inventor. Rumors were surfacing that the buildings, including his well-known lab, would be demolished for the development of condos. The group was running out of time. Matthew Inman, a web cartoonist known as *The Oatmeal*, hopped on board the campaign bandwagon and used his considerable audience to raise over $1.7 million in less than a week. With a mix of humor, satire, and a little education, he engaged tens of thousands of people around the world through his clever cartoons and videos to support the cause.

Like a traditional volunteer program, launching and managing a successful ambassador program will employ similar tactics. An organization starts by mapping out the program and benefits and then determines how to identify and recruit potential participants. This is followed by working to engage and retain the members as well as monitoring their activities.

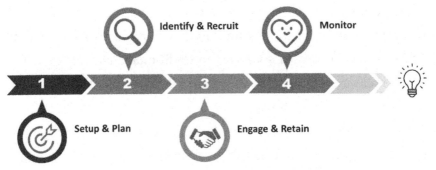

Step-by-Step Ambassador Program Overview

Program Planning and Setup

Utilizing the same approach as developing a project plan for a campaign (Chapter Five), start the planning process by outlining the ambassador program objectives and value proposition. What will members be asked to do and what will they receive in return?

In programs that we have launched, our ambassadors have been asked to do the following activities:

- Share news and information with their networks via social media, website, blogs or other community activities in which they are involved.
- Participate in one or more volunteer opportunity or local event.
- Distribute flyers for major events.
- Make a donation or become a member of the organization.

In return, our ambassadors have:

- Been featured on our website, social media, and in print newsletters.
- Received invitations to special events in which they are introduced to the crowd publicly or have been given a special "Ambassador" button to wear.
- Upon their annual renewal, they have received a welcome packet that contains freebies such as a lapel pin, sticker and pen, a "certificate of membership" that can be framed and displayed on a wall, as well as materials "hot-off-the-press" such as an annual report and new brochures. Other ideas might include t-shirts, ball caps, key rings, or mugs.
- In addition, they receive a monthly ambassador email with the latest news and sharing tips as well as an "ambassador spotlight" to encourage engagement.

It's important to outline the objective of the program with the expectations and benefits on a webpage for complete transparency. On this page, provide an online signup form. Consider creating a private online resources page or create a private group on Facebook where ambassadors can interact with one another and get instant information from the program administrators.

Determine the process for qualifying the ambassadors. Will they need to reside in a particular region? Would there be benchmarks set such as requiring a certain number of followers on social media or subscribers on YouTube? Might there be a limit to the number of ambassadors accepted into the program? Perhaps there would be additional criteria that involves diversity such as age, race, or gender.

As with any project or campaign, identify the key staff members and resources available for managing and communicating with the ambassadors on a regular basis. This would involve reviewing new applications, creating the communications via email or on Facebook, ensuring that ambassadors are invited to events and featured in print newsletters, and overseeing the freebies and perks associated with the program.

Identification And Recruitment

Outline steps for identifying and recruiting ambassadors for the program. These methods could include sharing the offer in print materials or in an enewsletter, posting an ad on social, or placing ads with external outlets. Flyers could be distributed at events or volunteer activities. Promotional videos might be created for distribution online or on-air.

One easy way to begin recruitment is to start by considering internal or existing groups. Perhaps there are a number of super-volunteers who have already been acting as ambassadors for the organization. The social media team may have a list of several individuals who actively engage with the brand and continually share and post news and activities. There may also be a group of donors or event participants who have voiced an interest in doing more for the organization.

In the early days of our ambassador program, I would take small brochures with me to networking events. Inevitably I'd be asked about my work and once I started talking about our community impact, most people would ask how they could get involved. *Voilà!* I'd give them an ambassador flyer. In addition, I would be sure to mention the ambassador program as often as I could at conferences or presentations.

Identification of ambassadors can also be aspirational. Are there local or national celebrities in the area who might be approached?

Do a bit of research to get a sense of their activities and interests. If they support similar organizations, they might be excellent candidates for an ambassador program. A "cold-call" will require a bit more preparation and may require a more formal proposal. Be prepared to provide information in the same way you might approach a donor meeting or grant submission.

Engagement and Retention

Just as a fundraising department engages, cultivates, and stewards donors and volunteers, ambassadors require the same kinds of strategies to keep them excited about spreading the word and participating in organizational activities. These strategies are very similar to other stewardship efforts for donors.

When they have participated in a successful fundraising campaign, loop them into the celebration! Ideas include:

- Highlighting ambassadors in social media and publicly thanking them for their efforts
- Inviting them to post-event celebrations
- Asking for their feedback and ideas
- Mailing copies of newsletters in which they were featured and include a hand-written thank you note

Ideas outside of a large campaign might include:

- Inviting ambassadors to participate in collaborative events and activities
- Asking them to join staff meetings or treat them to coffee
- Sending handwritten holiday cards
- Offering free tickets or admission to local productions, if available

- Collecting quotes or testimonials and using them in publications
- Considering opportunities for them to speak at external events or join a workshop as a panelist

One year, I nominated a few of our very active ambassadors for the "Volunteer of the Year" award which was presented at our staff day. They won. I asked them to come to the event without telling them why. They were nearly knocked out of their socks when their names were called for the award. At our staff day the following year, they brought us doughnuts!

Keep ambassadors at the forefront of your mind when planning organizational activities. The more they can be involved in the day-to-day activities, the more they will bond with your organization and continue to serve in a meaningful way year after year.

Monitoring

I've often been asked how to go about monitoring the activities of the ambassadors. How do we know that they are engaged and meeting the requirements? How do you control the messaging in case they say something incorrect, or worse, rather disparaging?

While there is no easy way to accurately tally the number of posts or shares of the group, there are many ways to monitor and track these activities. In general, ambassadors are looking for guidance and easy ways to spread the message. Providing them with scripted tweets and posts that include specific hashtags will allow for swift monitoring. Asking them to tag the organization will, obviously, notify the social media team of any activity. Providing fast facts will ensure that any blogs or editorials they write are accurate. Prior to any event or campaign, we crafted a "package" of approved talking points, facts, links and calls-to-action for the benefit of the group.

Encourage ambassadors to send the program administrators a notification or a link to anything they post online so that it can be shared by the organization. Also communicate that the program team or point of contact will be happy to provide editing services for anything they wish to write.

In the case of inaccurate information, I have found that ambassadors are completely flexible with making changes when an incorrect fact has been published. It merely needs to be brought to their attention. And, in nearly 10 years of managing an ambassador program, this happened only once.

In the case of a disparaging post, these same problems exist with board members, volunteers, and even staff members of an organization. Some readers may be familiar with the story of the Board Chair of the Corporation of Public Broadcasting who wrote an op-ed on why public media should be defunded by the federal government. Talk about an uproar. Other board members released their own op-eds chastising the Board Chair and calling for his resignation. In the end, public media was not defunded. The Chair did not resign. Life went on.

National organizations who have large celebrity councils have encountered issues when members run into legal or negative press. These individuals are simply removed from the council. If needed, a press release might be issued that addresses the separation between the organization and the actions of the individual. This scenario is a rarity. In general, an organization should always be prepared to handle negative publicity through a crisis communication plan.

Overall with this kind of program, the risks are minimal.

* * *

Launching an ambassador program harnesses the passion of supporters who believe strongly in the mission of your organization. It gives them the opportunity to give back in a unique way that honors and celebrates their advocacy efforts. In addition, it attracts new prospects, expands the awareness of an organization, and increases the activity of engagement and revenue campaigns. Plus, it's the final level of the growth funnel. And you can pat yourself on the back for a successful donor journey.

Even though it's been years since I managed the ambassador program at my former organization, I'm still in close contact with many of the folks who participated. We keep up with each other on social media. We meet for drinks and exchange Christmas cards. We bump into each other at networking events. So, in addition to all of the great benefits listed above, be prepared for the added bonus of this kind of initiative: making lifelong friends.

Memories of our lives, of our works,
and our deeds will continue in others.
—Rosa Parks

SECTION 4
THE
PERFECT POUR

Campaigns and Tactics

CHAPTER 10

The Bar Nuts

Engagement Campaigns:
Keep Them Coming. Help Them Stay.

The only sound in the room was the clock ticking in the distance. A stray bird chirped outside. Our small team of four sat around the conference table in silence. But it was not a dead silence, or a hold-your-breath anxious silence, or even an uncomfortable silence. We were contemplating. If there was an ultraviolet light or some gadget that measured energy pulses, the meter would have been swinging off the charts like a polygraph does when someone is lying. Wheels were spinning. Silent ideas were bouncing off the walls like ping-pong balls.

Our station had been given the opportunity to participate in a national pilot program for a peer-to-peer (P2P) campaign that offered a multitude of options but also presented some very complex layers that needed to be sorted out. It was a part-revenue, part-engagement campaign. There were restrictions on what we were allowed to edit within the website template provided to us.. The reporting was limited and the messaging was tricky.

"We can make it as big or as small as we want," I finally said. "It's a pilot … a test. And I want to be very cognizant of everyone's time and thoughtful of our resources."

We looked at each other. We chatted. We brainstormed. And we went big.

The interesting aspect of this campaign was that we created two simultaneous tracks targeting two very different audiences. One segment was designed to acquire and engage a younger, digitally savvy online audience. The other was aimed at transitioning a statewide fan club of older donors away from the traditional on-air pledge drive model to digital activities and fundraising. Both efforts were a heavy lift with unique challenges but also tremendous opportunity.

The platform itself offered the ability for individuals to set up a fundraising page and to issue participation challenges to friends and family. For example, "I love reading and challenge my friends to read two books this month." For every action people took on the platform, they could earn points and would be featured on the main leaderboard. We leveraged this point system to encourage more participation.

For the younger online audience, we created numerous "station challenges" for people to join and offered prizes and incentives for participation. The challenges were related to our brand identity and encouraged people to paint like Bob Ross, whip up a recipe from PBS Food, create a *Hamilton's America* karaoke video, or visit a location from a locally produced program, *NC Weekend*. The top five participants were featured in a weekly update email. The top 15 could win t-shirts and the top 30 were invited to a celebratory award ceremony at the conclusion of the campaign.

For the older fan club, we developed special giving days and managed their challenge pages. We created special on-air spots that aired around their show times and utilized their Facebook group for special announcements. The campaign culminated with a fan club luncheon featuring trivia and prizes.

Overall, we were the most successful station in the pilot program, raising over $25,000 with a reach of 2.4 million people. Did we hope for more involvement from our online audience? Yup. Did the older audience embrace the new digital model with open arms? Not initially.

Essentially, we made great strides in a new direction. Although the online group that participated most actively was relatively small, they were highly engaged and thrilled to show their excitement for the effort. And even though there was some strong resistance from the older audience, we were successful in introducing them to a new way of engagement and fundraising that 18 months later, really took hold and allowed us to build traction within the group.

Engagement campaigns are tremendously effective in keeping an audience active through the participation of activities. It's a way to mix things up and attract attention without having to continually send solicitations or circulate news and updates that may not be found particularly useful. It's an excellent way to keep the brand and mission at the forefront of the digital landscape. Engagement campaigns are like the free nuts at the bar. They are an added bonus for the patrons and the savory snacks encourage them to stay a little longer.

When evaluating the growth funnel, engagement campaigns span the entire range and can be used at any phase along the way. They can be exclusively focused on the acquisition of new audiences at the introduction phase. They can be utilized to cultivate lukewarm or curious groups. Obviously, they will lead to a conversion with opt-ins or contributions at the value exchange level. In our campaign example above, we even ended up pulling some of the participants all the way through the funnel from introduction to advocate. This group was so excited to be a part of the "winners circle" at the end of the campaign, they became tremendous ambassadors for our organization.

Let's examine some of the standard components needed for an engagement campaign as well as digging into a few tactics and ideas.

Standard Components, Tactics,
and Ideas for Engagement Campaigns

Standard Components

The themes of engagement campaigns are only limited by the imagination. But there are a few basic tools that need to be in place to have a successful digital effort.

- *Webpage or landing page that clearly outlines the campaign and call to action.*

    As explained in the next chapter, the CTA (call-to-action) for a revenue campaign is very clear: donate. With an engagement campaign, the CTA's differ. We might be seeking answers to trivia questions, looking for entries in a prize drawing, or as outlined above, participation in a challenge or activity. Therefore, it's vital to have all of the information about the initiative clearly defined on a webpage.

- *Email and social support to help continue the momentum.*
  Unlike a revenue campaign, the posts and updates of an engagement campaign can be very creative and enticing. With a participatory campaign, we might highlight the most active contributors. With a trivia campaign, we might regularly post the answers and promote the date of the next question. In the case of a drawing, we might post the winner and promote an upcoming drawing.
- *Ambassadors to spread the word.*
  Because of the light-hearted nature and often fun topics of engagement campaigns, advocates for an organization will be more than delighted to help promote the effort. These programs are discussed in detail in the previous chapter.

Tactics

In addition to determining what makes an engagement campaign appealing for individuals to join and participate, there are several additional tactics that can be employed.

- Partners: We might typically seek a monetary partner for a revenue campaign, but with an engagement campaign, the partnerships can be much more innovative. Consider a partner that would offer event space and additional in-kind partners for food, beverages or music. Partnerships can exist with other fan clubs or groups for boosting promotion, particularly in trivia campaigns. Partnerships with local gift shops or t-shirt vendors can be established for drawings or giveaways.

- Events: Hosting an "on-the-ground" live event is a great addition to an engagement campaign. It further fuels the cultivation phase of the growth funnel and gives an opportunity for networking and relationship building. In the campaign I outlined at the beginning of the chapter, we hosted three events. The first was a kickoff event at a local museum with music, a lively presentation, a photo booth, t-shirt sales, food and beverages. The second was an awards ceremony at the studio for the top participants with a tour, bingo, and framed certificates. The last was a campaign celebration luncheon at a local restaurant with our fan club members that included trivia and prizes.

- On-air spots or video promotion: Public media stations have the added benefit of incorporating on-air spots for their engagement campaigns but non-profits outside of this sector can take advantage of video promotion to enhance their campaigns.

- Prizes: People love to be rewarded for their efforts, so if the budget allows, creating an opportunity for a t-shirt or swag giveaway in an excellent way to boost interest in an engagement campaign. Partners who can contribute gift cards or other unique items can also be utilized in scenarios where budget might be limited.

Campaign Ideas

There are many amazing engagement campaign ideas and I'm sure that readers will know of or come up with hundreds of them. I'll outline a few of the high-level ideas we've implemented in the past.

Trivia Campaigns

There are a great number of people who are crazy about trivia and the topics are endless: science, history, food, sports, arts, geography, or animals among others. Consider pairing a trivia campaign with a drawing for a t-shirt or special gift box for a winning combination! Leading up to the live broadcast of the wedding of Prince Harry and Meghan Markle, we launched a series of "royal" trivia questions for the chance to win a "Regal Swag Pack." For our PBS Nerd online trivia month, we partnered with a pub quiz organization and toured several towns across the state making appearances with our swag, chatting with trivia enthusiasts, and collecting donations. Typically, our campaigns last for a few weeks with a rotation of questions. Participants answer them through an online survey form and answers are posted the following week on both email and social.

Content Campaigns

A content campaign could be a series of promotional videos, blogs or appealing emails paired with additional incentives for participation. Our station held a "Month of Memories" video campaign in which our talent and general manager recalled their best memories of public media. We launched these on YouTube and on-air, featured them in an email series, invited our audience to share their best memories, and offered the opportunity to win a "Time Capsule of Treasures" gift box. Leading into the year-end campaign, we held a fall food email series that featured timely recipes, fun crafts, programs or specials related to the food theme, and, of course, a chance to win a "Foodie Survival Kit!"

Content campaigns can be email only, such as joining the list for a weekly email of the best summer getaways, a series of recipes, or "six weeks of science." Encouraging the audience to sign up for specific content will guide them into the funnel and allow for additional mission-driven follow-up.

Ensure that the emails are appropriately branded and include a few words about the work of the organization to encourage further interest from the audience. Link to content within your digital eco-system so that the audience is not directed to external sites or content. Users should always see your branding or messaging with the opportunity to donate, volunteer, or participate in other ways.

Drawings and Giveaways

I've mentioned several drawings that we've incorporated into our engagement campaigns but there are certainly ways to host a give-away outside of a structured campaign. Occasionally we will simply offer tickets or t-shirts on social and ask participants to comment on the post for their chance to win. This boosts our engagement on the platform and helps to keep our content toward the top of the complex social algorithms. Drawings are perfect ways to engage audiences at events. Every year we have a presence at the State Fair and offer a giant prize basket. Participants simply enter with an email address which is collected on an iPad through a simple form. (Either SignUp Anywhere or Survey Monkey will work if the internal online system doesn't have a simple entry form.) We ensure that entrants are aware they will be added to our email list to allow for additional follow up and to promote email list growth.

One important note on this topic: a drawing or a giveaway is not the same as a raffle. It does not require a donation in order to enter. When a donation is required, this crosses the line into what could be considered gambling. In some states, raffles are permitted for nonprofit fundraising with certain limitations. Please be aware of your state guidelines when exploring the idea of a raffle or consider changing the entry requirements. Many nonprofits will allow entry into the drawing or raffle without having to make a contribution. This satisfies many state regulations and is common in sectors such as public radio.

To encourage additional support, add a donate button or link with a simple call-to-action in the email autoresponder of the entry form. For example, "Your support makes our work possible. Consider donating today!" This is a subtle reminder to those entering the drawings that we are a non-profit and support is necessary to continue our mission!

Photo Contests

Photography, like trivia, is another area with a high level of involvement and devoted fans. The photo contest we held was intended to last six weeks, but we received so many entries in the first few, that we had to truncate the campaign. From over 350 photos, we selected 12 to be featured in a year-end calendar. We utilized the photos in two ways: one for a small tri-fold calendar used in our direct mail acquisition campaign, and the other in a full-size calendar we used as an on-air fundraising premium, in our online member store, and as a year-end gift for our employees! The twelve winners were so excited to be selected, they posted announcements to their social platforms, essentially acting as ambassadors for our brand.

* * *

Because engagement campaigns span the growth funnel, they are an ideal tool to keep audiences moving level by level through the supporter journey. A giveaway can be an acquisition tool, a trivia campaign can be a cultivation touchpoint, and a photo contest can create a new pool of advocates. Promotion of these activities can boost social engagement and have a positive effect on the algorithms of the organization's social platforms.

These kinds of efforts create unique touchpoints outside of the standard contribution requests or newsletters, allowing for a unique mix of content that can attract attention from new audiences and delight existing supporters. Because of the creativity that can be utilized and extensive options available, engagement campaigns can show the personality of your brand and enhance the awareness of the work of your organization.

When developing engagement campaigns, consider what differentiates the organization from others who may be doing the same or similar work. What efforts will draw audiences in? What has been enticing or interesting about the mission or vision of the organization? What feedback has been received from supporters or volunteers on which a theme could be developed? A brainstorming session with team members from various departments will be a perfect way to outline some new ideas.

Contemplative, energized silences are welcome. Nuts provided free of charge!

Creativity is piercing the mundane to find the marvelous.
—Bill Moyers

CHAPTER 11

Caviar

Revenue Campaigns:
Serving Up the Very Best

It was 2008. Social media was just starting to become mainstream. Facebook had nearly tripled its growth to 145 million users. Twitter grew that year by over 752%. LinkedIn went global and boasted over 30 million members. Blogs were taking off like wildfire. Email marketing was ramping up.

In our area of North Carolina, social media events and Tweetups were appearing everywhere. The Triangle Tweetup had over 500 members and was booking major events at the State Fair and the NC Museum of Art. Raleigh was hosting Twestivals for charity and Ignite presentations packed the houses of music halls downtown.

It was the dawn of the digital age for nonprofits and we jumped on the bandwagon. I had just spearheaded the redesign of our website. I was dabbling in email communications and tinkering with content and scheduling. I explored everything I could think of in the social arena for our organization. We claimed our venues on

Foursquare. I used QR codes to enhance our warehouse tours. We hosted social media mixers with games and prizes. We live-tweeted events and posted them to Storify. We created Vines. I established our page on LinkedIn and set us up on Yelp. We started posting videos to YouTube and used Flickr for sharing photo albums. I cobbled together a small group of volunteers that grew into our Social Media Ambassadors program. I called all of this our "Virtual Village" and held presentations for our board members and partners on the amazing digital footprint we were creating.

Then one day I was giving a progress update to my boss and he said, "This is all great. But you need to make money."

It was one of those moments when the world comes to a halt. If there were a soundtrack playing, it would screech to silence. The characters of the movie would stare into the camera like deer in headlights. There would be a long, dramatic pause while the audience holds their breath. "Oh," I said, slightly puzzled and taking a deep breath, "okay." That was really all I could muster because I just didn't know what to say.

At the time I felt like I was starting all over from scratch. But in reality, I had the perfect setup for taking these activities to the next level. Up to this point, I had been working exclusively in the introduction and acquisition phases of the growth funnel. I had already developed a robust network of audiences. They were thoroughly engaged and had developed a passion for our mission. All I needed to do was create opportunities to allow them to show support through financial contributions and encourage a culture of peer-to-peer networking. In the years following, I created campaigns and events that took our organization from just under $150,000 in annual online giving revenue to over $1.2 million by 2016.

There was a lot of learning in those early years. The first few campaigns yielded tepid results. But I was determined and tenacious. Listening to best practices, learning from other organizations, attending webinars and conferences, and downloading as many whitepapers on email marketing and digital strategy that I could find, I figured out what worked for our audience. When I transitioned to another organization, I figured out what worked for that audience. While each organization required its own unique messaging, scheduling, and tweaks to campaign tactics, the overall strategies are similar and can be leveraged by any nonprofit, large or small.

Let's examine some of the standard components needed for creating revenue campaigns as well as digging into a few tactics and ideas.

Standard Components, Tactics, and Ideas for Revenue Campaigns

Standard Components

There are several types of common revenue-generating campaigns that range from long-term efforts spanning several weeks to one-day events with a quick impact. As outlined in Chapter Three, which examines the anatomy of digital campaigns, approaches can range from basic digital initiatives to full-blown integrated campaigns. More involved efforts require pre-campaign planning including the identification of target audiences (Chapter Eight), selecting items from the campaign toolkit to apply to the initiative based on the growth funnel strategy (Chapter Seven), and developing a project plan (Chapter Five).

As with engagement campaigns, revenue campaigns include the following standard components:

- A website landing page.
- Email communications.
- Social media support.
- Ambassador activation.
- If desired, website popup ads, video, and/or blog support.

Basic Tactics

In addition to the standard components, revenue campaigns will feature the following additional tactics that are typical to other fundraising initiatives:

Impact Statements

Think carefully about the impact statements for the campaign. How will these gifts make a difference? What will they fund? What is the impact of a dollar? Perhaps there is a particular program that the organization is aiming to support. Alternatively, it's perfectly fine to focus on the mission. If the campaign focuses on a specific program keep in mind that the gifts may have to be restricted. Most of the time, this is not a fun conversation with the finance department. However, broad language or generalized adjectives can be used to be specific but not require the restrictions. "Your gift will provide necessities for our shelter *such as* blankets and hygiene items" or "your gift will provide funding for your favorite programs *such as* Masterpiece, NOVA, and local coverage of events and activities." Spend some time crafting a powerful message.

Testimonials

For any campaign, testimonials are always a valuable and effective tool. Contact your sustaining members, major donors, ambassadors, or volunteers for statements either written or captured on video. To stimulate the conversation, ask questions such as:

- What does [our organization] mean to you?
- When you think of us, what comes to mind?
- Why do you support [our organization]?
- Why do you feel it's important for others to support us?
- Why do you think our services are valuable to the community?
- What are the top two or three services that you feel are the most important?

A Goal

Every revenue campaign should have a monetary goal. It will boost participation, increase excitement, and provide excellent talking points as the campaign proceeds and even concludes. For new campaigns, keep the goal to a reasonable, attainable number and build on it from year to year. This provides additional excitement the following year. For example, "last year we raised $5,000, this year we aim to raise $10,000!" Keep in mind that it's perfectly fine if the goal is not met. Language such as "we were so close but didn't quite reach our goal" might, and often does, generate additional donations after the campaign has concluded. (Refer to Chapter 13, Benchmarks and KPIs.)

Match Partner

Finding a corporate or business partner that will match campaign funds will always increase the success of a campaign. Donors actively respond to opportunities to double or triple the impact of their gift. While the matching funds may not always cover the entire campaign revenue goal, use phrases such as "our goal is $25,000 and your gift will be matched up to $10,000" to convey the same sentiment. When seeking match partners, be sure to clearly outline the benefits of the exposure they will receive. Some companies will utilize their marketing budgets for these kinds of contributions, so they will want to know the size of your email list and social audience, as well as the number of emails, posts or ads in which they'll be featured. To further extend the reach of your efforts, ask the partner to help promote the campaign to their audiences and networks.

Conditional Content

To avoid the hassle of having to create numerous segmented emails with targeted language and the possibility of members showing up on more than one list, consider utilizing conditional content in emails. In this way, only one email will be sent but, for example, group number one will receive a customized message and group number two will receive a different message. Conditional content is perfect for donors vs. non-donors. Ideally, if the email system is sophisticated enough and the data is reliable, emails should be as personalized as possible. Incorporate a first name, perhaps a county or city, donation or volunteer history, or other types of group participation that will make your donor feel special. (See Chapter Eight on segmentation and personalization.)

Donation Form

Of course, a donation form is essential for a revenue campaign. Ideally, a separate form is created specifically for the campaign to allow for proper branding and messaging while the main, generic donation form remains active. Remember that not everyone in the digital space might be aware of the campaign. Someone visiting the website out of the blue might find the campaign messages confusing. Keep campaign donation forms linked to campaign promotion such as specific website features, social media ads, and emails. As for tracking results where highly specific post-campaign analysis was necessary, I would create three or four duplicate forms that would be used for individual marketing promotion. (Note: Appending source codes to URLs can also be used if the form reliably captures this information.)

Dynamic Ask Strings

A tactic for increasing contributions is to create dynamic ask strings from donor history, should the online giving system offer this feature. Utilizing the last or largest gift, an ask string will be customized to more closely align with a donor's giving capacity. So, if a donor's largest gift is $25, the ask string might show $15, $25, $40, or $60. On the other end of the spectrum, if the largest gift was $500, the string might show $375, $500, $625, or $1,000. The support team for the online giving system should be able to help with this level of customization.

Campaign Ideas and Strategies

Once the basics are in place, it's time to get creative! Will the campaign be long-term or just one day? Does the campaign align with a holiday or national event? Is there a local or national partnership or event in which a campaign could be created? The possibilities are endless!

Year-End Holiday Campaign (A Long-Term Effort)

Typically, a year-end holiday campaign will span from six to eight weeks depending on the priorities of the organization. The challenge with these types of campaigns is keeping the momentum going so that the audience doesn't drift away from lack of interest. It's important to mix engaging content with campaign asks, to use a variety of platforms for content distribution, to segment audiences appropriately, and to strike the right balance with scheduling messages so that they are neither annoying and repetitive nor distant and forgettable. Keep an eye on the email, social posting and ad performance to tweak the strategy as the campaign progresses.

An eight-week email series will be a rotation of captivating content but will always include some sort of reminder about the campaign. While some charities send more than one email a week or even a few in one day, this is a schedule that I found worked well at my former organization:

- Week 1: Campaign kickoff. Email is focused exclusively on the campaign. Conditional content can be used so that non-donors receive an ask while recent donors are asked to share.
- Week 2: Newsletter with organizational activities. Campaign promotion is secondary, sometimes at the bottom of an email.

- Week 3: Letter from the President/CEO about the importance of the campaign.
- Week 4: Typically Giving Tuesday focus. Multiple emails around this day. Heavy messaging focused on goal updates.
- Week 5: Blog post or other engaging content. Subtle campaign promotion.
- Week 6: Staff holiday greeting card or video. (No campaign promotion but add a donate link in footer.)
- Week 7: Campaign update featuring goal thermometer. Utilize "almost there!" language.
- Week 8: Two, perhaps three, emails. Campaign update featuring testimonials. Heavy focus on the goal status. Also, utilize "Last chance to give" language on Dec. 30 or 31.

At most non-profits, the messaging strategy for a holiday campaign will focus exclusively on the holiday theme for the duration of the campaign. However, in public media, there is an on-air fundraiser (pledge drive) window held nationally right in the middle of the campaign as well as a direct mail effort, so the tactics and messaging shift slightly. Fundraisers can use a combination of these efforts to create an integrated initiative that makes sense for their organization (see Chapter Three on integrated campaigns).

To accommodate the promotion needed for the drive and the direct mail campaign, there is a shift in tactics. Instead of focusing on newsletters or blog posts, I feature a "holiday food and program series" during the eight-week campaign time frame. This aligns with the season, allows for promotion of relevant programming, and points to affiliated websites. (PBS Food, for example, features a donate button localized for the station.) As mentioned in the previous chapter, I strongly advise against pointing to external content where the user can get lost in another organization's mission or activities. Remember to keep all content relevant to the organization pointing to the organizational website and social accounts.

- Week 1: Fall holiday food series email #1. Features: recipes, special fall programming, a drawing for email acquisition, kids' crafts. Large donate button at the bottom pointing to a special donation form.
- Week 2: Fall holiday food series email #2. Similar content pointing to same donation form.
- Week 3: On-air fundraiser/pledge drive promotional email. Features special programs. Points to a custom donation form for the drive.
- Week 4: Giving Tuesday. Multiple emails around this day, focused on goal. Separate donation form for this effort.
- Week 5: Winter holiday food series email. Features: recipes, programming, crafts or other local events. Donate button points to the same form used in the food series.
- Week 6: Two emails: Staff holiday greeting card or video. Launch of year-end campaign.
- Week 7: Campaign update featuring goal thermometer.
- Week 8: Two emails: Campaign update featuring testimonials with "almost there" language. "Last chance to give" on Dec. 30 or 31.
- In addition, on January 1 we send an email for "Healthy Resolutions" day—our on-air virtual drive featuring self-help programs.

In addition to the year-end or fiscal year-end campaign, there might be other long-term campaigns that last several months. In our community, a large foundation offers a sizeable match for a campaign that spans a three-month time frame. In this case, occasional but consistent messages are important. Regular reminders through a variety of platforms should be sent but not posted so often that they are perceived as harassment or badgering. The audience will quickly become tone-deaf and ignore the messages completely. Bi-weekly reminders sent for the few weeks leading up to the deadline of the campaign are appropriate. When reaching the deadline, the most effective strategy is to capitalize on the "almost there" or "last chance" language, and increase the communications.

Giving Tuesday

As most fundraisers know, Giving Tuesday is a "global day of giving" that follows Black Friday and Cyber Monday. The benefit of holding a Giving Tuesday campaign is that organizations can capitalize on the national focus of this initiative. The challenge is being heard above the noise. Thousands of charities hold Giving Tuesday campaigns, so how does an organization compete?

I have found success in setting a goal and focusing the messaging on the status of the goal for the duration of the day. In addition, performance will be boosted by having a match partner or even multiple partners. One partner who will match up to $20,000 or four partners who will match $5,000 each really makes no difference to a donor who is excited that their gift will double in impact.

As for promotion, there are many organizations who start promoting Giving Tuesday very early in November. In a traditional year-end digital campaign, the initiative will kick-off at the beginning of the month, so the promotion for Giving Tuesday can actually detract from these early, but very important, campaign communications. At a public media station, there is competition for promoting the end-of-November on-air (pledge) drive. The balance for these promotions will be dependent on other marketing needs.

In general, I've found that soft promotion of Giving Tuesday starting in mid-November through email newsletters or posts on the website work well. Heavy promotion starting the Friday or Saturday before and leading right up to Giving Tuesday is generally very effective. On Giving Tuesday, I've sent two emails and relied most heavily on social promotion and ambassadors for updates throughout the day. At our public media station, we also promote Giving Tuesday on-air as part of the drive.

Holiday Honor Campaigns

Launching a campaign on a day when a donor can honor a loved one is a great way to boost contributions throughout the year. Valentine's Day, Mother's or Father's Day honor campaigns can be fun and engaging for donors. Map out the timing of the campaign so that there are no delays with fulfillment. For example, if the promotion centers around the honor recipients receiving a special greeting card for the holiday, allow for plenty of time to mail the cards.

At one time, there was popularity with eCards, or email greeting cards to honor recipients. Over the years, spam filters have caused more problems with this type of feature than actual benefit to the donor.

A Giving Day

Celebratory days such as National Cat Day, Take-a-Hike Day or Public Media Awareness days that are aligned with an organizational mission can be crafted into a giving day campaign. Consider creating fun memes, trivia, giveaways or live videos to enhance the engagement of such campaigns.

Live-Streaming Event or Telethon

Public Media fundraisers are generally rooted in on-air (pledge) drives but traditional nonprofits can take advantage of these kinds of campaigns through a partnership with a traditional media outlet or by using live-streaming platforms. (See Chapter Nine for success we've had with an online "telethon.") Live-streams can be held in short intervals or longer events that feature interesting content to encourage donations. Ideas include music, tours, interviews or other types of performances that will captivate the audience and keep them tuning in.

As with Giving Tuesday, utilize email promotion, online ads, heavy social coverage on Twitter, and ambassadors to get the word out to keep the momentum strong.

Social Fundraisers

A spin-off of the telethon idea is to hold a social-only fundraiser that utilizes Facebook, You-Tube live or even Instagram TV tools. The live moments require highly engaging content that may be location-based or reveal interesting features of an event.

In one of our social fundraisers, we mapped out a series of locations that were a part of one of our local broadcast programs. In one day, we traveled to the three locations, toured them, and interviewed the guests and owners. In each of the segments, we promoted a t-shirt drawing and gave updates of the fundraising goal. Pre-promotion, including online advertising, is essential for a social fundraiser in order to build excitement for the day.

* * *

Crafting digital revenue campaigns can be an exciting aspect of the overall fundraising portfolio for an organization. The results are real-time, the momentum can build quickly on social, and tweaking initiatives for future efforts can be an enjoyable exercise for the whole team. It's a gratifying experience to move your existing social and digital audiences who are already invested in the organization through the levels of the growth funnel to deepen the relationships. And, it's often fulfilling for audiences to know that they are supporting your organization in a relevant and meaningful way through online channels.

For digital revenue campaigns, it's important to follow best practices, to regularly analyze results, and to build a campaign calendar for future growth. Before, during, and after a campaign, make notes of successes or challenges and take screenshots for reporting purposes, particularly if external partners are involved. Ensure that you have a strong system in place for thanking your donors, ambassadors, and partners. It's a vital part of fundraising!

With all of these tools in hand, you'll build your digital campaign efforts into a strong and steady source of revenue for the organization. And your audiences will certainly appreciate the "caviar" you offer!

Genius is in the idea. Impact, however, comes from action.
—Simon Sinek

CHAPTER 12

Happy Hour and Daily Specials
Prospecting and Recapture

It was our monthly 8:00 a.m. marketing committee breakfast meeting and we listened as the Development Director gave her fund-raising updates. I quietly sipped my foamy latte and calmly nibbled on my bacon and avocado omelet but as she filled in the details of her efforts, my mind was racing and my chest was getting tight.

"Here is my list of prospects for the grant and I know y'all have seen this before. They're the major donors from last year and I'm working on asking them to upgrade their gift to qualify. But don't worry, I'm being nice so that they'll take my call," she smiled sweetly.

The grant which she was referring to was a $50,000 matching challenge for donations from new or lapsed contributors or upgrades from existing donors. The timeframe for raising this money was four months. I had worked with this grant at my former organization, but we had a significant acquisition strategy. It was so strong, in fact, that we didn't even need to count lapsed or upgraded gifts. Gifts from new donors always met the grant expectations by the deadline.

But this was a much smaller organization with an operating budget a quarter of what I had worked with in the past. There were only a few weeks left and they had only raised half of what was needed.

"We're also having our part-time intern make calls to donors and reaching out to area churches," she glanced at her notes. "Most of them are receptive to hearing about the challenge but we're not getting a lot of direct contributions. And our marketing coordinator has been posting to Facebook but the impressions and shares are going down."

I took a slow, measured breath to calm my anxiety. The approach she was taking felt like wheels spinning in a muddy, desolate field. There was no tactical plan for soliciting new prospects or recapturing lapsed donors. She was repeatedly calling the hot leads and even worse, asking existing major donors to upgrade, over and over.

The discussion turned to how to approach these folks next year to get them to upgrade again for the same challenge. I nearly choked on my omelet.

What this organization needed was a structured prospect and recapture strategy. Sure, reaching out to major donors to ask for an upgrade is great, but unless there is a written confirmation or verbal commitment to these funds, they can't be counted on to fulfill the entire grant. In fact, after a few years, these donors are going to reach capacity. They will get sick of being harassed or they will feel that their gift is not truly appreciated. Either way, this will damage the relationship. Given the time it takes to develop these partnerships, this is a dangerous and potentially destructive practice.

What we needed to do was set up a "happy hour" to entice new prospects and issue a few "daily specials" to recapture our wayward audiences.

In Chapter Seven, we touched on numerous tactics for acquisition and stewardship through the growth funnel. Prospecting tactics fall within the first three levels: introduction, cultivation, and acquisition. When focused on recapturing or renewing our donors, the tactics fall within the value exchange and stewardship areas of the growth funnel. The above example illustrates the importance of not only feeding the beginning of the funnel but ensuring that lapsed donors are returning.

Prospecting

In the Growth Funnel, tactics such as websites, social media, blog posts and advertising are a few common acquisition practices. Websites provide the general public with information about the mission of an organization and the importance of its services. Someone coming to a nonprofit website should be able to quickly ascertain the basic intent of the entity, in addition to quickly locating the donate button. Social media goes a level deeper in providing online users with more details of these efforts, including inspiring stories and pertinent updates. Blog posts can capture the hearts of the public and advertising can catch the attention of a wide audience.

In addition to these basic tactics, there are numerous strategies that build on these activities.

Google Ad Grant

Google offers a grant of $10,000 per month in free ads for nonprofit organizations. While it does require an investment of time to setup and manage the account, the benefits for driving traffic to the website or to highlight a featured initiative is tremendous. With my former organization, I was able to determine through source code tracking that we received tens of thousands of dollars a year in donations through Google traffic after launching our Ad Grant.

Here is a basic overview and a few high-level tips for setting up a new account:

- The $10,000 is allocated daily through campaigns. If there is one campaign, the daily amount available is $329. At my current organization, I set up three campaigns. One is for organizational ads, another for engagement such as campaigns or special initiatives, and a third for program promotion. Depending on the importance of the effort, the campaign amounts can be reallocated. For example, if we were focused on a big fundraising initiative, I might allocate $134 per day on the "engage" campaign and reduce the organizational campaign to $105 and the program promotion to $90. These amounts can be changed at any time.

- Within the campaigns, ad groups are established. This is where topics are clustered together into groups that make sense. For example, ad groups might be based on campaigns at different times of the year, specific programs or initiatives, email signup, volunteer solicitation, events, and mission-driven or topical categories.

- The ads themselves reside in ad groups. Creating ads can be intimidating and hard to understand. My suggestion? Go to Google and search for ads of other organizations or topics that you're considering promoting. This will help with understanding the structure of Google ads and generate new ideas. Additionally, look at the copy on the landing page of the website and replicate the language based on main themes or concepts. For each new ad group, I recommend three to four ads. Let them run for about two weeks, then check their performance. Deactivate the ads that are not performing at a five percent or higher click-through rate. Sometimes there will be only one ad in an ad group that has stellar performance and that's completely fine.

- Each ad requires a number of keywords. In general, I brainstorm 10-15 keywords and see how they perform. After about a week, I log in to tweak the keywords, both deactivating the low-performing ones and adding new ones based on Google suggestions.

There are a number of additional features that Google offers to help make nonprofits make their ads more successful. Take the time to research the suggestions and components before activating them. Google wants nonprofits to be successful and they have a plethora of resources. Follow the "Google Ad Grants" YouTube channel for more tips and tricks to optimize every penny of the $10,000 per month offer.

YouTube Giving

Upon registering for "Google for Nonprofits" to apply for the Google Grant, organizations have a number of benefits such as G Suite, increased space on Google drive, access to the Google Maps API and publishing benefits, as well as YouTube Giving.

As of the writing of this book, YouTube call-to-action overlays and donation cards have been deactivated. But, YouTube is in beta testing for a host of new donation features including campaign embeds, community fundraising tools, matching gifts, and chat-for-good. Keep an eye out for that!

Facebook Ads for Prospecting

Facebook offers a variety of options for targeting ads. For a small investment of $50 to $100, an organization can make quite an impact with an enticing ad. For prospecting, there are a few targeted strategies to consider:

- Uploading external lists

  There are times when an email list might be made available to an organization but, because there was no formal opt-in process, the emails cannot be uploaded to the email platform (*see reference to CAN-SPAM laws at the end of this chapter). In one advertising partnership we had with a local media station, they sent a promotional email on our behalf and, as a bonus, we received the list of email addresses of people who opened it. Perhaps a direct mail vendor has access to email addresses when purchasing lists for acquisition mailing. Utilizing Facebook ads is a perfect way to establish the connection with these prospects. *Public Media stations should be taking advantage of the PBS prospect names and emails that are collected from localized interactions on the PBS platforms!*

- Lookalike audiences

  Select or upload a target list, then select a "lookalike" audience. Facebook will create a new audience that is similar to those on the original list or from the original source. Ensure that the ad has an appealing call-to-action and avoid asking for donations.

When creating Facebook ads for prospecting, remember that these groups might be unfamiliar with the organization's mission and, therefore, not prepared to make a monetary investment. Consider the ideas in Chapter 10 for engagement campaign suggestions such as drawings or giveaways, trivia, interesting email updates, or contests.

Peer-to-Peer, Member, and Ambassador Efforts (aka Referrals!)

We touched on peer-to-peer efforts in Chapter 10, and Chapter Nine takes an in-depth look at the power of an ambassador program for acquisition. Utilizing existing, active members and partners to help grow the donor base is an authentic approach that not only expands the mission but also offers a secondary engagement benefit for these advocates of the cause.

Consider these ideas:

- Membership or Community Challenges

   In this effort, donors are asked to make a gift and then "challenge" their peers and community members to do the same. The organization provides a number of assets to make it easy to spread the word. These can include email templates, social posts, printable letters, or phone scripts. Consider a campaign in which members are asked to "Pledge Five" and personally contact five of their peers to make gifts. Expanding that further, communities could compete with each other in a membership challenge with a website leaderboard that reflects the results as the campaign progresses. (A sophisticated online platform is not necessarily needed for a leaderboard. A tally of the donations and a daily update to the website would make this fairly easy. Messaging can indicate that results will be posted every day at noon.) In the example above of our Development Director repeatedly calling major donors for an upgraded gift, imagine how much more successful these calls could be if she asked them to participate in a "Pledge Five" or membership challenge instead. The donors would feel valued and helpful while the organization's prospect list grows.

- Peer-to-Peer Campaigns

   Along the same lines as a community challenge, a peer-to-peer campaign taps into the network of a donor or participant. (See Chapter One for details about P2P platforms.) Utilizing an online website, participants are asked to create a fundraising page on behalf of the organization. In a walk-a-thon or fun run, a page would be created to sponsor the walker or runner with a gift. Campaigns could be created around experiences such a "polar plunge" event, a dog walk, or baking contest. In our community, participants can rappel down the tallest building in the city if they raise $1,000 each. In a birthday campaign, the participant asks for donations to the organization rather than a birthday gift. This could be replicated for weddings, holidays, or special occasions.

- Ambassador, Major Donor, and Board Support

  Similar to the ideas above, very engaged groups of supporters such as ambassadors, major donors, or board members are asked directly to share the work of the organization with their network of friends or family. In a holiday or year-end campaign, development officers might create packets that contain ready-to-mail letters and pre-stamped envelopes for these groups to easily mail. Postcards and small brochures can be distributed for them to share. Perhaps the organization posts flyers in community centers or coffee shops about an upcoming event. These groups can also be utilized for speaking engagements or tabling events. Social media ambassadors would be asked to share through their online platforms.

Online Advertising with External Partners

Nonprofit organizations can often negotiate reduced-cost and in-kind advertising with media outlets, particularly local news and radio. These packages can be bundled in a variety of ways to have significant impact. As mentioned above, we partnered with a local news outlet to enlist their help in promoting our year-end campaign through their email list. During on-air fundraising drives, we rotate through a variety of program promotions to boost the visibility of the campaign with online advertising and we coordinate radio ads during the same timeframes.

Events and Tours

For events where an organization has a table or booth, there should always be an opportunity to collect email addresses. The challenge is making this enticing for the visitors. Having a sheet of paper on a clipboard and asking for an email address is rarely successful. Consider offering a giveaway or drawing. This could include a gift basket filled with goodies such as tickets to an event, coupons to local restaurants, books, mugs, gift cards, or institutional items such as t-shirts or hats. We found that a prize wheel will capture attention and encourage people to stop by. To make email collection easier, consider using an iPad with a service such as SignUp Anywhere, Survey Monkey, or a form provided by the CRM. Make sure that there are very clear disclaimers that people will be signing up to receive emails.

In addition to a tabling event, organizations can host an event or tour that requires registration. A simple tool such as EventBrite allows an organizer to send targeted messages to their attendees and, through those communications, follow-up actions can be initiated to establish a relationship.

ProTip! For additional event promotion, consider posting the event to Facebook with a link to the EventBrite page for registration. While EventBrite offers decent event exposure through their platform and emails, posting the event to Facebook will significantly expand the promotion to a wider audience.

Traditional Mail Acquisition

While development officers may have strong feelings about traditional direct mail practices, the ROI clearly shows that mail still works. Building a robust mail strategy includes acquisition campaigns. Names from lists such as magazine subscriptions, association memberships, or public records are used to create a strong acquisition list. It's important to remember that the initial ROI on an acquisition list is low but the success lies in the long-term value of the new donor. Acquisition mailings feed the funnel, resulting in a steady flow of new donors.

Recapture

While acquisition tactics are necessary for all nonprofit organizations, they can be time-consuming and expensive. An equal amount of time, if not more, should be focused on re-engaging lapsed donors and recapturing audience attention.

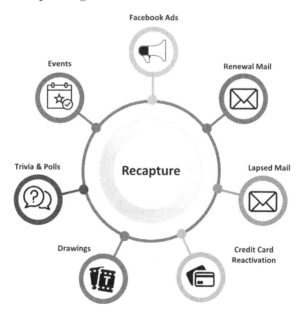

The Association of Fundraising Professionals, in conjunction with the Center on Nonprofits and Philanthropy at the Urban Institute, launched a program called the Fundraising Effectiveness Project to help charities evaluate their efforts and make smart decisions about their strategies and initiatives. In their most recent analysis of over 9,000 nonprofits nationwide, they discovered that overall donor retention has declined from 50% five years ago to now just 46%. Additionally, only two out of 10 new donors repeat their gift (23% retention rate), while six out of 10 existing donors give again (60% retention rate).

Essentially, if an organization has a total of 10,000 donors, at a 46% retention rate, less than half of them will return in year two. In five years, they will have only 205 donors. If these 10,000 donors are new, at a 23% retention rate, they will have only six donors by year five. If these are $50 donors, year one will produce a nice $500,000 addition to the budget. But by year five, this will have dwindled to a mere $300. I don't know any fundraiser who wants to report that to their Executive Director!

Consider these tactics for recapturing lost donors:

Facebook Ads for Recapture

In addition to running Facebook ads for prospecting, they can also be used for recapturing the attention of audiences whose interest has started to fade. Consider these options:

- Low or no action from emails: A robust email platform should have the ability to track the activities of users who receive emails from the organization. Within our system, we regularly export email addresses of people who have opted-in to our emails but have not opened them in a year or more and upload this list to Facebook for targeted ads.

- Opt-out email lists: In the same format as the low or no action email group, exporting an opted-out email list to serve them Facebook ads in a great way to keep them connected with the organization.

- Membership renewal or lapsed lists: If the organization has a renewal or lapsed mailing effort, consider a Facebook ad to target the accounts with email addresses to further support the campaign. Utilize the same or similar branding for a coordinated and cohesive approach.

The content for recapture ads should generally include a specific call-to-action in which the user provides information that will reactivate their account. We might entice them with a giveaway, send a campaign message, or notify them of an event. Consider a series of ads over a few weeks that rotate between news, interesting activities, or new videos. If featuring the latest blog post, include links on the landing page for volunteer signup, the ability to donate, or directing them to join the organization's social media platforms. If there is an enticing publication featuring articles such as recipes, healthy living tips, or the latest research on the endangered Mississippi Gopher Frog, require an email address to download the information. Utilize a sign-up form to volunteer or to attend an event.

ProTip! Following the call-to-action, ensure the confirmation pages have some sort of follow-up step that will further engage the individual. From a volunteer form, add a link to donate. If a donation form, add a link to follow on social. (See Chapter Seven on growth funnel strategies!)

Traditional Lapsed or Renewal Mailings

Organizations with a robust direct mail program will most certainly have a lapsed campaign effort to reengage donors who have not made a gift in over a year or more. Mailings could be generated up to four times a year to recapture these contributors. In smaller organizations that may not be able to afford a large-scale effort to all lapsed donors, a cost-efficient mailing to high-dollar lapsed donors could have a big impact. For membership organizations, renewal mailings are a must. It's typically wise to mail a donor whose membership is about to expire a month or two before the expiration date and then send several follow-ups afterward. In many public media organizations, this can comprise up to nine mailings: three before expiration, one notice of expiration, and then five to follow up. This might seem shocking to many organizations, but the numbers speak for themselves. The membership renewal campaign at our organization brings in double the revenue of our direct mail: $3 million vs. $1.2 million.

Lapsed or Renewal Emails

In tandem with Facebook ads, consider incorporating email reminders to any audience who might be receiving mail. Stick with the same branding for coordination and consistency. Donors who receive contribution notices by mail, email, and through reminders on Facebook are more likely to give. As discussed in Chapter Three, integrated campaigns perform 60-68% better than siloed efforts.

Credit Card Reactivation

Organizations should be focused on encouraging monthly contributions over one-time gifts. They offer a steady stream of support and reduce the cost of expensive giving reminders. However, cards often expire without the donor's knowledge or they may have a lost or stolen card and forget to reactivate their contribution. In many cases, nonprofits are losing thousands of dollars a year due to expired or declined credit cards.

Consider these tactics for credit card reactivation:

- Automatic Email Reminders: Most online giving platforms will have the ability to trigger an email reminder when a card is declined or expired. Ensure that these reminders, as with all automatic email communications, are well-branded and include custom language appropriate to the organization.
- Phone Calls: Some donors overlook important emails, so a phone call might be helpful. At our organization we phased out telemarketing efforts and utilized the service of the vendor to call donors about their expired credit cards. This initiative resulted in tens of thousands of recaptured gifts per year. Internal teams or board committees could also be established to make calls a few hours a week.
- Mailing: If these efforts fail, consider a mailing to reach out to these donors. As with lapsed mailings, if the organization is tight on budget for full-scale outreach in this way, segment the list to mail the highest-level donors for the most impact.

Giveaways, Drawings, Trivia, Polls and Events

Enticing members, donors, or followers with a giveaway or encouraging them to participate in trivia is an excellent way to keep your members active and engaged. Utilizing these efforts for the purposes of re-engaging or recapturing their attention is simply a matter of segmenting and targeting audiences through various marketing efforts to reach lapsed donors and members. A history museum might launch a trivia campaign in coordination with their current exhibit. An animal rescue organization could host a puppy tour as a recapture event. A civil rights organization might launch an opinion poll targeted to a specific interest group. An environmental group could utilize a photo contest to recapture donors and members. Refer to Chapter Ten for more engagement ideas and strategies.

* * *

Many of the campaigns and tactics for prospecting and recapturing audiences overlap but the key is to target them with specific messaging that resonates with the individual. In prospecting, the messaging will be focused on informing the audience of what the organization does within the community or region. In recapture efforts, messaging will focus around a reminder of the importance of the mission and encouraging a renewed investment.

When determining the goals and outcomes for a large campaign or grant, such as the one mentioned at the beginning of the chapter, set realistic and clear expectations. For example, if the organization needs to raise $25,000, revenue from prospects might account for 20% of the goal, recapturing or renewing lapsed donors could account for 50%, and upgrading existing donors might account for another 30%. Consistent reporting will be necessary. And, while there may be some tweaking along the way, the team should feel nearly 100% certain that these efforts will be effective before investing internal resources into what could be an all-consuming campaign.

Organizations with strong prospecting and acquisition strategies will ensure that a steady stream of funding keeps flowing through the growth funnel. It's the Happy Hour of fundraising! And just as offering daily or weekly specials keep customers coming back to an establishment, engaging in consistent recapture or renewals efforts will ensure that donor commitment and partnerships continue long into the future. Both components are vital to the financial health and growth of an organization.

> *'Build it and they will come' only works in the movies.*
> **—Seth Godin**

CAN-SPAM laws prevent the practice of sending unsolicited or deceptive messages. Violations can result in massive fines but more often result in the "blacklisting" of an email server, which means all emails will be rejected by the receiving servers.

SECTION 5
THE AFTER PARTY

The Post-Campaign Activities

CHAPTER 13

Closing Time
Tracking Metrics, Benchmarks and KPIs

"Oh my gosh, this is so exciting ... where are we now?" she exclaimed as I refreshed the screen of recent donations and calculated the totals toward our goal amount. Our Creative Director was volunteering as talent for our on-air fundraising drive and, on this night, we were heavily pushing the message of reaching a monetary goal. I was busy tallying the gifts in between our live breaks. We were just a few hundred dollars away from it. The staff and volunteers were on pins and needles.

Having lived through hundreds of campaigns where we came down to the wire just before the deadline, I had nearly forgotten that sense of pure adrenaline that comes with tracking real-time donations for a live fundraiser. It occurred to me that rarely do our colleagues and counterparts get to experience the intoxicating feeling of such an event. This is one of the joys of fundraising. One of the reasons that people are attracted to this line of work. To know that your message and the mission of the organization is so inspiring that people will willingly give a gift of support with their hard-earned dollars is likely one of the most rewarding experiences one will ever know.

Once the party is over, the lights have dimmed, and the proverbial door to the campaign has closed, it's time to dig into numbers to determine the effectiveness of our efforts. Staff members, executive leadership, and donors alike will be waiting with bated breath to know the results.

While there are hundreds of metrics one can use to evaluate a campaign, I have found that, in general, time is of the essence. Unfortunately, as one campaign ends, another task is right on its heels. A new campaign, budgets, personnel, contracts, database issues, meetings, calls, emails … the list goes on and on. In order to avoid "analysis paralysis" and ensure that other activities keep rolling, I've found that the below benchmarks and KPIs are the most essential and effective.

Revenue & Giving	Marketing-Comms	Overall Effectiveness
• Overall $ • # of Gifts • Avg Gift Amt • New Donors • Existing Dnrs • Sustaining+Ad Gift • Highest Gift • Lowest Gift	• Open Rate • Click- Thrus • Email Gifts • Social Posts • Online Ads	• Increase over Last year • Conversion Rates • Cost Per Dollar Raise

Campaign Metrics, Benchmarks, and KPIs

Revenue and Giving Evaluation

- Overall Revenue: Total number of all dollars raised. If evaluating an integrated campaign, I would advise separating online, offline, on-air, and corporate dollars. Even drilling down into email, social, and website gifts might be helpful. This will help accurately establish the goal for the next campaign.

- Number of Gifts: Total number of all gifts. This number will identify any anomalies such as a major gift of $5,000 in a campaign with a goal of $10,000. As mentioned above, segmenting the revenue by channel will be helpful for future planning.

- Average Gift Amount: Overall revenue divided by number of gifts. This will, again, identify anomalies in giving. Looking at the channels will give a better idea of the giving patterns for online or offline. For example, it might be discovered that there are more online gifts at lower gifts amounts while there are fewer offline gifts, but they are at higher gift amounts.

- Number of New Donors: This determines the effectiveness of acquisition efforts for the campaign.

- Number of Existing Donors: This indicates the effectiveness of motivating donors to continue to support your mission.

- Sustaining Donors Making an Additional Gift: Gold stars for gifts made in this category! This shows that the campaign message was so inspirational that a committed, ongoing donor contributed even more.

- Highest Gift and Lowest Gift: These benchmarks are helpful in setting the giving levels for future campaigns. Looking at the number of gifts within ranges will also drive these decisions. For example, one campaign might have 50% of the gifts in the $25-50 range while another might have 50% in the $100-$200 range. Utilize this data to determine where to start your ask strings.

Marketing and Communications

- Email: Open Rates, Click-throughs, and Gifts. The open rates will determine if your subject line was effective. Click-throughs will indicate whether your content was appropriate. Looking at the number of gifts and the revenue amounts from the email will indicate a successful conversion.
- Social Post: Impressions, Clicks, Shares. Impressions will give an indication of the overall ad performance and how often it appeared on-screen. Clicks would show that the user was interested. A share is the gold standard: the user was inspired enough to forward it to their network.
- Online Ad Performance: Impressions, Clicks. Similar to social. Impressions show ad performance, clicks show interest.

Overall Campaign Effectiveness

- Increase over Last Year: This may be common knowledge for most readers, but I include the formula because I have been asked about it in the past. If A is last year and B is this year, here is how to calculate the percentage of increase over last year: $(B - A) \div A * 100$. For example: Last year $4,500 was raised. This year $7,750 was raised. $(7,750 - 4,500) \div 4,500 * 100 = A$ 72% increase! Nice work!
- Conversion Rates: This metric will indicate how successful your efforts were in converting visitors to donors. Divide the number of donation form visitors by the number of donors. If there were 1,200 visitors with 500 donors, the conversion rate would be

41%. (500 ÷ 1200 * 100). To drill down even further, consider setting up a separate form used only by marketing efforts on the website, by email, and by social to calculate the conversion rates for each channel.

- Cost Per Dollar Raised (CPDR): The cost to raise a dollar will indicate if you're campaign expenses were in line with the amount of money raised. Simply divide expenses by the amount raised. Let's say the campaign raised $27,500. The expenses were $4,600 and included printing, room rentals, food, online processing fees, and equipment. 4,600 ÷ 27,500 = only $.16 to raise a dollar! (Typical CPDR rates for a fundraising program range from $.20-.25. Events might go up to $.50, major gifts or planned giving might be only $.10. Mail acquisition, which focuses on the long-term three to five-year impact of donor, will initially be a loss in the range of $1.00-$1.25 to raise a dollar.)

* * *

In addition to the celebratory atmosphere that comes with tracking these numbers, it also helps audiences feel more invested and involved with the campaign. At our 24-hour live-streaming telethon, we'd have ambassadors and volunteers come to the warehouse "studio" during the last hour of the event, just to experience the excitement and to witness the last few minutes before the campaign came to an end. Results should be shared widely with staff members and supporters alike, even in a case where the goals were not met. Many times, these messages will spur even more gifts after the campaign deadline.

From setting realistic goals for future campaigns to determining the effectiveness of a campaign for evaluation, tracking these numbers year after year will give the organization the appropriate benchmarks and KPIs to make smart decisions for campaign planning.

> *There are no secrets to success. It is the result of preparation,*
> *hard work, and learning from failure.*
> **—Colin Powell**

CHAPTER 14

The Local Hangouts
Networking and Training

I walked through the door into a room full of strangers. A friendly woman at a table greeted me and handed me a nametag. With a marker, I filled out the blank space below "My name is..." and wrote *Jen @CharityJen*.

It was 2008 and I was attending my first Tweetup. I ordered a drink from the bar and meandered through the groups of people talking, laughing, and simultaneously tweeting. My mind was speeding at a mile a minute. What was I really doing there? What is CharityJen anyway? What is my brand, my platform? I wasn't a consultant, I wasn't trying to get new clients, and I wasn't even there to represent my nonprofit in an official manner. This was truly an exploratory mission. A bit of a learning experience, so to speak. I was there to try to understand Twitter and how people used it for their work, either personal or business. I was aiming to make connections. But how to explain that in a two-minute introduction to people obviously so far advanced on the platform scrambled my mind a bit. It was a classic social anxiety situation.

I smiled pleasantly and made eye contact with people passing by, desperate for any invitation to join in a conversation. My stomach clenched in knots and I took many deep breaths, wondering if I should just finish my beer and head home. But I stuck with it and after an agonizing 15 minutes or so, I found an equally uncomfortable individual. We struck up a conversation. Slowly others joined us until we had a nice group of about five people chatting comfortably. We made our connections on twitter, posted some "nice to meet you" tweets, and headed home.

Following this rather curious event, I went on to attend more tweetups, more social events, breakfast meetups, luncheons, presentations and workshops. Not only was I learning as I went along, I was expanding my personal network and that of the nonprofit for which I worked. These authentic and organic conversations at "local hangouts" led to the creation of our ambassador program and the launch of several successful fundraising and engagement events. I met experts who gave us advice on Google Ads, SEO, and provided us with basic marketing tips. Through these connections, I was invited to present at association meetings and conferences, participate in panels, and join local boards.

Making connections with people in the community can lead to creative event ideas, new collaborations, in-kind contributions, volunteer assistance, or even new donors. I remember going to an SEO event and after the presentation, I struck up a conversation with a couple who were seated at my table. I listened as they told me about their new consulting business and their struggles getting things off the ground. Then they asked me about my work. I explained our new digital initiatives and similar struggles getting our things off the ground. "How can we help?" they said with genuine interest. I didn't have to ask for a thing! They offered assistance without hesitation.

There is no better way for an individual to grow personally and professionally than getting out there and meeting fellow professionals, community advocates, and like-minded individuals. These kinds of events offer the space to practice an elevator pitch and get comfortable with questions such as, "what do you do, what are your interests?" They help us keep abreast of new community initiatives and activities. It allows one to be informed of the latest trends in various industries.

Here are a few groups that I have found most valuable in my career so far…

National Associations
Dust off that suit coat or spiffy blazer

Association of Fundraising Professionals

The AFP works to ensure fundraising best practices by supporting members through training and education, conferences, research, and reports. The AFP focuses on ethical fundraising, advancing philanthropy, inclusivity, innovation, and collaboration. There are chapters across the U.S., Canada, Mexico, Africa, and the Middle East.

afpglobal.org

Chapter locations: *afpglobal.org/chapters*

NTEN

The Nonprofit Technology Enterprise Network, most commonly known as NTEN, focuses on helping nonprofit professionals utilize technology to help improve the mission of their organization. Online discussions revolve around topics such as websites,

CRMs, digital communications and inclusion, cybersecurity, the cloud, project management, and metrics. Educational resources include reports, fellowships, digital cohorts, blogs, and events. Local clubs are scattered across the U.S.

www.nten.org

Clubs and groups: *local.nten.org*

Young Nonprofit Professionals Network

YNPN works to empower emerging leaders by providing resources, fellowships, conferences, and a community network of young individuals active in the nonprofit field. There are over 40 chapters across the U.S. and in Canada.

www.ynpn.org

Chapter locations: *www.ynpn.org/chapters*

National Council of Nonprofits

The largest network of nonprofit organizations, the National Council of Nonprofits provides support and advocacy for charities across the country. Independent chapters work to connect nonprofits by providing webinars, conferences, town halls, and job opportunities in the nonprofit sector.

www.councilofnonprofits.org

Chapter locations: *www.councilofnonprofits.org/ find-your-state-association*

American Marketing Association

The AMA focuses on cutting edge marketing solutions through extensive research, scholarly journals, and case studies that contain expert strategy. Through events, podcasts, certifications, and interactive tools, they cover advertising, branding, engagement,

marketing communications, and digital. Conferences are offered nationwide through both the national office and local chapters.
www.ama.org
Chapter locations: *www.ama.org/pages/FindChapter.aspx*

Public Relations Society of America

PRSA aims to enhance the careers of communications professionals by providing leadership training, certifications, online communities, and events. They also focus on ethics, diversity, and advocacy. Both national and local chapters offer job opportunities in the communications sector.
www.prsa.org
Chapter locations: *prsa.org/network/Chapters/Find*

Finding Local Networking Groups
Have some fun and meet new peeps!

Meetup

Meetup is a platform for like-minded individuals to get together to engage in shared-interest activities. Meetups can range from a casual lunch at a local restaurant or coffee shop to more formal clubs that meet at a large venue with presentations from local experts. The website makes it easy to find events based on a variety of topics. Groups typically meet on a repeat basis.
meetup.com

Eventbrite

Eventbrite is used for more formal events or conference registrations, as the platform has a robust ticketing feature and email capabilities.
eventbrite.com

Facebook Local

Facebook Local is a mobile app that makes it easy to find events that are posted to Facebook. While many of them might be more along the lines of concerts or community activities, it is still a valuable tool for identifying networking opportunities. *facebook.com/local/*

Publications and Nonprofit News
Stay informed and on top of the latest developments

Chronicle of Philanthropy

A resource for essential news about the nonprofit industry, coverage of current events, reports of new studies, and educational opportunities such as webinars and toolkits. Articles cover the gamut of nonprofit leadership, finance, strategy, fundraising, major gifts, grants, and technology. Free enewsletters are available. Access to premium articles and the monthly print editions are available for an annual fee. *www.philanthropy.com*

Philanthropy Journal

An online publication that offers feature stories, valuable resource articles, weekly nonprofit news digests, and a podcast. Access to all content, including newsletters and articles, is free. *philanthropyjournal.org*

Nonprofit Quarterly

Nonprofit news coverage with articles focused on management, governance, public policy, and philanthropy. Print editions along with access to premium articles and webinars are available for an annual fee.

nonprofitquarterly.org

Center on Nonprofits and Philanthropy at the Urban Institute

In-depth research on nonprofit trends and performance to help organizations increase effectiveness and impact.

urban.org (Click on Policy Centers to find Nonprofits and Philanthropy)

Direct link: *urban.org/policy-centers/center-nonprofits-and -philanthropy*

NextAfter

A research and consulting firm that helps nonprofits expand their reach, grow their donor file, and increase revenue. Most of their studies incorporate valuable digital strategies. They offer training, webinars, and hold an annual summit.

nextafter.com

Blog: *nextafter.com/blog*

Summit: *niosummit.com*

Nonprofit AF

Not only is this blog funny and heartfelt, it will give anyone a boost on even the worst days in a nonprofit professional's life. Vu Le covers serious topics with a pinch of humor and it's a joy to read his posts.

nonprofitaf.com

Life begins at the end of your comfort zone.
—Neale Donald Walsch

Conclusion
Raise Your Glasses

I remember giving a birthday card to a colleague of mine a number of years ago. On the front was a cartoon woman smiling at her desk while everything around her was on fire: the computer, the phone, the trashcan, her entire cube and the door. The caption said something like "Welcome to hell! How can I help you?"

There is absolutely no doubt that there are accomplishments to celebrate within nonprofit work: moments of triumph and success, excitement for events and fun activities, heartfelt conversations with donors and community members, laughter with colleagues, and joy within the meaningful impact of the mission. But at the same time, the day-to-day grind can feel like the world is on fire. We are flooded with emails, meetings, calls, mailings, data processing, social posting, events, reports, or budgets and that doesn't even account for fundraising efforts, planning, or growth initiatives.

I've written this book to act not only as a reference guide, but also as a testimony to show that these things *can* be done. Digital fundraising campaigns *can* be implemented in the face of adversity.

Organizational silos *can* be broken down for effective collaboration. Anxiety about online activities *can* be overcome. Setting up a team for success by expanding resources and recruiting ambassadors *can* happen in a seemingly resistant environment.

It's not always easy. But with persistence and determination, it *can* be done.

When I first launched the food bank's Twitter account in 2009, our CEO would snicker every time I mentioned that I was posting. I would walk through the warehouse and my colleagues would tease, "oh, so you're *tweeting* again, Jen?" They thought my QR codes were weird and pestered me about wasting time on social media. That was until they saw the increases in online revenue: over $100,000 every year through 2016 when I left.

At our public media station, fellow development officers were anxious and sometimes downright angry about the new strategies I was introducing. I felt like I was pushing a monumental boulder uphill. At one point, I had to have a meeting with some of the leadership and patiently explain "this is what you hired me to do... online fundraising." Every day, I took a deep breath and would try again. And again. And again ... until our success was not only reflected in revenue growth and engagement, but also featured in blog posts, webinars, and conference presentations by PBS for the entire public media system.

Change of any kind is going to feel disruptive and intimidating. And the change-agent is going to take the heat. Finding strength through the examples in this book, understanding the tactics to present clarity around plans, and being able to define terminology will help provide the tools for success. Keep this book on a nearby shelf. Grab it when a colleague wanders by with a look of confusion on their face as to what it means to launch an integrated campaign. Refer to it when tensions rise during the planning of a new initiative with another department. When it's time to outline goals for the new year, pull in a few of the engagement efforts to keep priming the pump for new prospects.

But a word of caution: this book should not be used as the sole reference point for introducing these practices at an organization. I cannot stress enough the importance of networking with peers and continued learning. This field is like no other in a traditional development department. Digital moves fast. Very fast. We all may be celebrating the incredible impact of our Facebook posts until algorithms change and destroy our carefully constructed plans. New announcements are made daily. We must pay attention. Subscribe to the publications I recommend in Chapter 14, follow the blogs, and get out there to meet fellow colleagues. It will help make your efforts more impactful, more creative, and may even act as a bit of therapy for you and your stressed-out colleagues.

For some of us, we may be fortunate enough to work in an environment with the freedom to experiment and a team supportive of new initiatives. What a dream! Sections three, four, and five will be your lifelines. Others may not be so lucky. Resistance, confusion, and a bit of heckling might be our reality. In either case, keep in mind the overall goal of this field: digital growth. It's imperative that we cultivate online audiences and strengthen our digital fundraising efforts to contribute to the revenue portfolio. While the platforms and tools may change in the coming years, we know that future generations are online, living and breathing digital media and communications, and we need to be prepared to meet them where they live.

The most important part is to begin. To start somewhere. Make moves. Shake things up, however so slightly.

And when we are down, and frustrated, and just about sick of trying to push that doggone boulder uphill, remember those moments of magic and inspiration that captivated us from the very beginning. Those moments that remind us why we work so hard for our nonprofit organizations. Why we try day in and day out to make things better in the world around us.

I vividly remember watching truckloads of donated sweet potatoes being poured into bins and thinking of the thousands of families who would have meals that night. Kids going to bed with full bellies. Parents with a bit of relief, however fleeting. The homeless man who came to the shelter for a meal and continued to volunteer years later, even though he worked two jobs to make ends meet and barely had enough time to rest. The woman who clutched her little girl in her arms as she waited in line for hours to get a bag of groceries, her face tired and defeated but hopeful for that bag of food. The animal shelter staff members who breathed a sigh of relief as my daughter and I cleaned and prepped the kitty rooms for adoption days. The woman who teared up as she explained that she learned how to read because of the educational shows she watched on her public media station. The cheers of the volunteers and staff members at the end of a 24-hour fundraising event when we reached our goal.

This is the beauty of charitable work. The ultimate target toward which we aim. The fuel that allows us to persevere and succeed, despite the challenges. May the stories and concepts in this book offer inspiration and support for your future endeavors.

My best wishes to you, my friend. With martini in hand, I salute your efforts!

> *We could never learn to be brave and patient,*
> *if there were only joy in the world.*
> **—Helen Keller**

Connect with me at charityjen.com/insiders for more resources, tips, and helpful information.

Thanks for being awesome.

Appendix
Key Takeaways by Chapter

Chapter 1 - Building the Menu
Defining Digital Channels and Categories

Objective:

Understand digital engagement and fundraising. Engage audiences online to encourage participation and move prospects through the growth funnel from a mildly interested individual to an active donor and champion for the cause.

Distribution Channels:

The platforms used for digital support of these efforts including websites, blogs, social media, audio and video hosting platforms, email, and apps.

Tactics:

The tactics used to support digital engagement and fundraising efforts are defined into four categories: digital content, digital marketing, digital fundraising, and digital operations.

Digital Content:
The creation and production of information consumed online.
Types of content include: photos, video, live-streaming, infographics, news and information, articles, publications, audio (podcasts).

Digital Marketing:
The intentional promotion of content and activities.
Tools include: online advertising, promotional emails, pre-roll video, pop-up promotions, SEO, data analytics, surveys.

Digital Fundraising:
Building creative and inspiring campaigns with the above tools to obtain monetary support.
Initiatives include: personalized messaging, optimized donations forms, impact statements, clear call-to-actions, partnerships, sponsors.

Digital Operations:
The technical aspects of managing platforms and production services.
Activities include: website and email development, graphic and video file delivery, app and API management, analytics dashboards, email automation.

Chapter 2 - Launch
The Importance of Digital. And Taking Risks.

Objective:
Understand the importance of digital initiatives and taking risks despite the possible anxiety and intimidation of online efforts.

Instant Results. Thrilling Campaigns.

Online fundraising offers the ability to share real-time results and an authentic transparency of the process. Supporters can share in the excitement of the campaign and help celebrate its success. The flexibility allows for immediate pivots should the effort need an extra boost or quick improvement.

Diversify Revenue with Digital

A diverse portfolio, including a digital fundraising portfolio, is vital for the financial health of organizations. Large nonprofits will reach new and younger audiences. Small nonprofits can benefit from the quick response and excellent ROI.

Reaching Younger Generations

The "young'ns" are online, they are on social, and they live and breathe the web. Nonprofits need to adopt new strategies to reach them while simultaneously cultivating their existing donors. Digital fundraising is the key.

Pro-tip

Don't use a period when texting.

Chapter 3 - Meat of the Matter

Anatomy of Digital & Integrated Campaigns

Objective:

Understand the options of various digital and integrated campaigns by utilizing a roadmap of the tactics.

Basic Digital

Used for short campaigns with quick impact such as one-day fundraisers. Used to provide exposure for a

longer campaign. Can also support an offline effort.
Components: Email, Social Posts, Ads on
Facebook, Instagram, or Twitter.

Robust Digital
Used for digital campaigns or initiatives
that require more online exposure.
Includes the basic components: Email, Social Posts/Ads
Plus: External advertising, promo video, blogs, Facebook live
ads, Instagram stories, email with conditional content, donation
forms with dynamic ask strings, and/or website popups.

Integrated Campaigns
Used to join multiple fundraising efforts during a
similar time frame into a cohesive, multi-channel
promotional and marketing campaign.
Includes all of the digital components above
with print, on-air, and mail efforts.

Chapter 4 - Shake It Up
Navigating Org Charts, Silos and Lanes

Objective:
Encourage collaboration between departments to develop
a healthy culture resulting in project success and allowing
room for new initiatives, including digital fundraising.

Listen. And communicate.
Initiate a listening tour, hold meetings that encourage
open dialog, assign "buddies" or communication partners,
or enlist a coach or mediator. Discuss reporting structures,

ensure that department goals and priorities are clear, share projects in the pipeline, and outline lacking resources.

Collaboration

Establish a shared mission or goal. Encourage an idea-sharing environment opening the floor to all opinions. Determine project plans and timelines to ensure accountability and ownership. Share successes to encourage future commitment.

Restructuring

Consider the possibility of reorganizing, shifting workloads, or creating new departments or divisions. Leaders must regularly evaluate the success of projects and initiatives and pivot when necessary for continued collaboration.

Warm Fuzzies

Allow staff members to interact in an unstructured setting. Host social occasions, field trips, volunteer opportunities, or holiday parties. Issue awards and certificates. Allow for family members to join in picnics or hikes.

Chapter 5 - Ingredients for Project Success
A Canvas. A Toolkit. A Playbook.

Objective:

Utilize tools that outline objectives, deliverables, resources, and cost analysis to ensure efficient and effective planning and communication for campaign or project success.

Project Plan

Utilizing a business model canvas helps develop a clear strategy for an effective initiative. The areas to develop include key partners, activities, and resources, value propositions, customer relationships and segments, channels, cost structure and revenue streams. The campaign toolkit will be helpful when discussing resources and channels.

Campaign Toolkit

A comprehensive list of the basic needs, marketing assets, and strategic approaches needed for efficient and focused planning of any initiative.

Playbook

Serving as a roadmap for campaign or project planning, the playbook outlines the details to create team alignment and ensures effective communication. A comprehensive playbook should include objectives, goals, impact statements, timelines, marketing and promotional outlines, event details, partners, and main contacts. Post-event successes or areas of improvement and financial outcomes will be helpful for future planning.

Chapter 6 - 86 the Turnover
Advocating for Resources

Objective:
Create proposals that advocate for more resources to improve efficiency, support organizational growth, reduce turnover, and create a healthier, lower stress environment.

Basic Plan
Uses an "if this, then that" concept such as "if we have these resources, then that is how things will improve." Presents the benefits of the investment while outlining consequences of business as usual.

Complex Plan

Identify objectives: Relate areas of growth to the mission, vision, or high-level priorities of the organization.

Gather internal data: Utilize SWOT analysis to establish the current landscape and identify areas of growth and opportunity.

Research external data: Seek sources such as national surveys and sector data to craft support for the plan.

Determine ROI and KPIs: Outline the overall impact and measurement for success.

Know the Audience

Prepare the plan in ways that will resonate with the group or individual based on overall traits such as analytical, creative, formal or casual. Be prepared to answer follow-up questions based on larger factors the group will have to consider.

Chapter 7 - The Funnel Flow
Grow Your Audience. Deepen Relationships.

Objective:

Clarify the strategy of fundraising and marketing efforts in phases or growth levels. Keep the team focused on long-term goals. Encourage creativity to grow the audience and deepen relationships.

Phases

Basic categories can be as simple as capture, convert, nurture or partner. Others include exposure, influence, engagement, and action. We examine six phases…

Introduction

Builds mission awareness, helps people understand what we do. Includes social media, website, blogs, podcasts.

Cultivation
Motivates an individual to join, view content, or learn more.
Includes social engagement, event
interaction, retargeting campaigns.

Acquisition
Compels an action, encourages a user to opt in or become a fan
Includes online participation, email opt-ins, on-air fundraisers.

Value Exchange
Activates a donation or a volunteer sign-up.
Includes volunteers, donations, enewsletters,
member publications.

Stewardship
Deepens the relationship through
recognition and acknowledgment.
Includes thank you letters, donor visits, tours, member benefits.

Advocates
Repeat engagement, a brand ambassador, or greater investment.
Includes major or planned donations, board
participation, sustainers, repeat volunteers.

Chapter 8 - Special Seating
Defining Audiences through Segmentation and Personalization

Objective:
Create personal connections with constituents by utilizing
segmentation and personalization plus the importance
of data hygiene to make these efforts successful.

Common Donor Categories for Segmentation

Monthly or Sustaining Donors

First Time Donor

Donors by Level or Gift Size

LYBUNTS or SYBUNTS (Last year or some
previous year but not this year)

Lapsed or Deep Lapsed Donors

Board Members

Volunteers and Ambassadors

Regions, Interests, Age

Communication Preferences.

Segmentation Strategies

Ensure that personalization addresses
the categories of the donors.

Recognize the ongoing support of sustainers.

Applaud the participation of volunteers and board members.

Ensure that prospect messages include the
mission and impact of the organization.

Utilize regions and interests to craft
specialized campaign messages.

Data Hygiene Efforts

Develop standard practices and data-entry rules and procedures

Perform ongoing duplicate checks

Promptly handle account requests

Utilize external services: NCOA checks or data screenings

Chapter 9 - The Regulars

The Power of an Ambassadors Program

Objective:

Increase mission awareness and community impact by utilizing the personal and professional networks of ambassador partners. Extend and boost the marketing of the organization. Drive action for campaigns, attract new prospects, and increase revenue.

Program Planning and Setup

Outline program objectives and value proposition.

Utilize: Informational webpage, signup form, resources page.

Offer: Welcome packet, freebies, membership certificate, event involvement, recognition.

Communicate via monthly email or Facebook group.

Identify internal staff members to facilitate program.

Identification and Recruitment

Market the program through enewsletters, online ads, flyers, video.

Recruit via internal connections, super-volunteers, social media, donors, or event participants.

Utilize networking events. Consider celebrity outreach.

Engagement and Retention

Keep ambassadors engaged and participating: Collaborate through events and activities, join staff meetings, highlight on social media, solicit feedback and new ideas, use quotes and testimonials in publications, offer free tickets, send personalized thank you notes, treat them to coffee!

Monitoring

Provide talking points, fast facts, links and scripted tweets with event hashtags. Request a tag for the organization and notification of anything posted so that it can be reposted by the organization. In the case of inaccurate information, contact the ambassador to make changes. In the event of a larger issue, activate the necessary crisis communication plan.

Chapter 10 - The Bar Nuts

Engagement Campaigns: Keep Them Coming. Help Them Stay.

Objective:
Engage a new or existing audience, diversify messaging to gain continued interest, and keep the brand in the spotlight touching all levels of the growth funnel.

Standard Components
Website landing page, email communications, social media support and ambassador activation.

Basic Tactics
Partners: Consider an event partner for in-kind food, beverages, music, or venues. Fan clubs to boost participation. Local vendors for drawings or giveaways.
Events: Hosting an event offers networking and relationship building in an intimate environment.
On-air spots or videos: Utilized to enhance campaign promotion.
Prizes: Boost interest and excitement with t-shirt or gift card drawing.

Campaign Ideas
Trivia Campaigns: Can be hosted online or at an in-person event.

Content Campaign: A series of videos, blogs, or emails of captivating information paired with incentives for participation such an email signup or giveaway.

Drawings and Giveaways: Can be a part of an existing campaign or stand-alone to boost social or event engagement.

Photo Contest: Generates excitement among participants and photos can be used by the organization for additional promotional efforts such as premiums and social.

Chapter 11 - Caviar

Revenue Campaigns: Serving up the very best.

Objective:

Raise revenue through online, digital campaigns.

Standard Components

Website landing page, email communications, social media support and ambassador activation. Can also include website popup ads, video or blog support.

Basic Tactics

Impact statements: How will the gifts make a difference?

Testimonials: Capture written quotes or video statements.

A goal: Will boost participation and increase excitement.

Match partner: Find matching funds to double or triple campaign gifts.

Conditional content: Allows for cleaner segmentation and more personalized messaging.

Donation form: Utilize clean, branded forms specifically linked to marketing efforts for accurate tracking.

Dynamic Ask Strings: A customized way to
align with the donor's giving history.

Campaign Ideas and Strategies
Year-End Holiday Campaign: Long-term six to eight
week effort to maximize year-end giving.
Giving Tuesday: A one-day "global" giving effort that requires
creative marketing to stand apart from other charitable efforts.
Holiday Honor Campaign: A one-day campaign
for gifts that honor a loved one.
Giving Day: Spin-off of Giving Tuesday but themed
to align with the organizational mission.
Live-Streaming Event or Telethon: Using live-streams
(Facebook, YouTube) for fundraising efforts.
Social Fundraisers: Effort completely on
social, streaming, tours, or interviews.

Chapter 12 - Happy Hour and Daily Specials
Prospecting and Recapture

Objective:
Ensure a steady stream of donors and revenue flow into
the organization by engaging in consistent prospecting or
acquisition efforts and recapturing lapsed donors and members.

Standard Components:
Websites, social media, blog posts, advertising.

Prospecting Tactics
Google Ad Grant: $10,000 per month in free Google ads.
YouTube Giving: Forthcoming video fundraising tools.
Facebook Ads for Prospecting: Create targeted ads to external

lists uploaded to the platform or create lookalike audiences. Referrals via Peer-to-Peer, Member, or Ambassador efforts: Create membership or community challenges, launch P2P campaigns, utilize engaged groups such as ambassadors, major donors or board members to spread the word. Online Ads: Negotiate a reduced-rate or in-kind advertising package with media outlets. Events and Tours: Utilize these efforts for email collection. Traditional Mail Acquisition: Purchase outside lists for targeted mailings to bring in new donors.

Recapture Tactics

Facebook Ads for Recapture: Create targeted ads to emails with low or no activity, opted-out lists, or lapsed and renewal lists. Traditional Lapsed or Renewal Mailings: Schedule consistent mailings to lapsed donors and launch regular renewal letters to expiring members. Lapsed or Renewal Emails: Coordinate Facebook ads and follow-up emails in conjunction with mailings for an integrated campaign that reaches individuals through a variety of platforms. Credit Card Reactivation: For recurring or sustaining donors with a declined credit card, set up email notifications, create a team for making phone calls, or arrange a mailing to notify them of the issue. Giveaways, Drawings, Trivia, Polls and Events: Utilize these engagement tools for recapture campaigns by segmenting the audiences appropriately.

Chapter 13 - Closing Time
Tracking Metrics, Benchmarks, KPIs

Objective:
Establish analysis practices in order to evaluate the effectiveness
of a campaign, set realistic goals for future campaigns, provide
results to donors and partners, and encourage excitement
and involvement of staff members and volunteers.

Revenue and Giving Evaluation
Overall Revenue Totals, Number of Gifts, Average Gift Amount,
Number of New Donors, Number of Existing Donors.

Marketing and Communication
Email: Open Rates, Click-throughs, Gifts.
Social Posts: Impressions, Clicks, Shares.
Online Ad Performance: Impressions, Clicks.

Overall Campaign Effectiveness
Increase Over Last Year, Conversion
Rates, Cost Per Dollar Raised.

Chapter 14 - The Local Hangouts
Networking and Training

Objective:
Grow professionally and personally by getting
involved with organizations, attending trainings,
and learning more about the field.

National Associations
Association of Fundraising Professionals
NTEN: The Nonprofit Technology Enterprise Network
Young Nonprofit Professionals Network
National Council of Nonprofits

American Marketing Association
Public Relations Society of America

Finding Local Networking Groups
Meetup, Eventbrite, Facebook Local.

Publications and Nonprofit News
Chronicle of Philanthropy
Philanthropy Journal
Nonprofit Quarterly
Center on Nonprofits and Philanthropy at the Urban Institute
NextAfter
Nonprofit AF

Acknowledgments

I wrote a quote on a sticky note and posted it to my office computer. It said, "You can. You should. And if you're brave enough to start, you will." Someone covertly came to my desk and crossed out the "IF." It gave me the strength to push through the worst of times this past year, personally and professionally.

During the writing of this book, I was learning to live life on my own in a new city while navigating a divorce after 19 ½ years of marriage. I hit a deer on a four-lane highway going 70 miles per hour, at night, alone. We had to put down our sweet 16-year-old family dog. I had a debilitating case of bronchitis. In addition, after a long, exhaustive, and painful battle with metastasized breast cancer, my mom died.

Essentially, I have a lot of people to thank for helping to make this book possible.

To my dad, Galen Longenecker, who, while struggling to navigate life after nearly 48 years of marriage to the woman he loved unconditionally, was simultaneously my on-the-ground personal promoter and avid supporter. A true salesman and my personal champion, I owe him everything.

To my amazing daughter, Madison Newmeyer, with whom I laughed and cried, shared face masks and music, and munched on late-night Mellow Mushroom pizza while binging Netflix shows. Who painted touching pictures for me, and who, at 6:00 a.m., walked to the corner store for fresh spring water to make me the best possible cup of French-pressed coffee on one of the most difficult days of the past year. "It's just you and me and the moon." My love. She shines like the sun.

To my sister, Amy Longenecker Brown, who offered constant support and encouragement even while handling a bustling household of toddlers—my beautiful niece and nephews: Esmé, Felix, and Oliver. Her creativity and determination are truly astonishing.

To my "career dream teamers" with whom I've experienced so many exhilarating successes and learned so many professional lessons throughout the years: Shannon Falter, Cathy Miller, Amy Etheridge, Brenda Peterson, Christy Simmons, Linda Fisher, Jennifer Caslin, Molly Rivera, Carter Crain, Tivi Jones, Sarah Grieco, and JC Polk.

To Maxine Oakley for her encouragement, support, listening ears, and for being a true friend through all of the ups-and-downs of life, both in and out of the office.

To Sally Wade, my personal cheerleader and my most enthusiastic advocate, for giving me my first public presentation opportunity in Raleigh and AFP board appointment, as well as being the most lively and spunky person I've ever met.

To my amazing social-media-ambassadors-turned-friends: Gregory Ng, Ilina Ewen, Lisa Sullivan, Joe Mecca, Shana Overdorf, Deirdre Reid, Sue Anne Lewis, and Joshua McKinney. Special thanks to Shana who encouraged me to join her board and serve the homeless of Wake County, if only for a short time. And to Greg who had a wild idea for a 24-hour live-streaming telethon in 2012 that helped reimagine the possibilities of fundraising in the digital space. Not to mention his trusted wingman Mike Adams. And to Sue Anne, who was hell-bent on breaking the world record for the largest food drive in 24 hours ... and did it.

To Diane Moyer and Andrea Lehman, two of my closest and trusted high school friends with whom I shared those breathless, remarkable teen years and with whom I still share the curious twist and turns of life, particularly this past year.

To Rob Newmeyer who knows the backstory of most of these anecdotes more than anyone. Supportive, encouraging and willing to participate in any of my wild ideas back in the day, we created a mountain of memories and one extraordinary daughter.

To Susan Scott for giving me the opportunity to spread my wings, for having endless faith in my abilities, and for offering emotional support during some of my most trying times.

To Peter Werbicki for teaching me how to dig into numbers and develop well-forecasted budgets.

To Ashley Delamar for helping me see beyond my perceived boundaries.

To Anne Swartz who shared in my excitement, helped pre-edit the book and, without hesitation, dropped everything to provide encouragement whenever I needed it.

To Dave Horne and Linda Fineman for their enthusiasm, positivity, and hard work to transition their NC EastEnders Fan Club audience toward online activities. And for helping to make PBS Nerd a great success!

To Kivi Leroux Miller, Antoinette Kerr and all the folks associated with Bold & Bright Media for taking a chance on a first-time writer, and for their openness and enthusiasm for this body of work.

To Christer Berg of Portraits with Purpose for an outstanding collection of gorgeous headshots.

To Mrs. Janet Banks, my high school English teacher, who gave me the confidence and encouragement to write, even though it took exactly 30 years for something to come of it.

To the Piccolo Man, the delightful fellow who made me laugh, wherever he may be.

And to my Mom ... the sweetest soul I've ever had the pleasure to know. I was beyond fortunate to learn patience, style, and grace from her. She taught me how to listen—although she listened to me more than I did to her. She taught me kindness and compassion. She helped me see the beauty in everything, while she saw it in everyone around her. While I never had the chance to share this book with her, I know she is looking over my shoulder with pride and delight.

References by Chapter

Foreword

Care2, hjn and NTEN. 2019. 2019 Digital Outlook Report - Navigating the Unknown. Care2, hjn and NTEN. http://www.care2services.com/hubfs/2019%20Digital%20Outlook%20Report/2019%20Digital%20Outlook%20Report.pdf

Chapter 2 – Launch

Frailey, Kerstin. 2017. "What Does the Nonprofit Sector Really Look Like?" Guidestar Report https://trust.guidestar.org/what-does-the-nonprofit-sector-really-look-like

Perry, Mark. 2014. "Fortune 500 Firms in 1955 vs 2014…" AEI Report. http://www.aei.org/publication/fortune-500-firms-in-1955-vs-2014-89-are-gone-and-were-all-better-off-because-of-that-dynamic-creative-destruction/

Joslyn, Heather. 2018. "How a Maverick Tapped Into a Wellspring of Giving" The Chronicle of Philanthropy. https://www.philanthropy.com/article/Charity-Water-s-Founder/244652

Harrison, Scott. 2018. THIRST: A story of redemption, compassion, and a mission to bring clean water to the world. Charity-Global, Inc. Reference to bankruptcy, chapter 29 page 191

Feltman, Rachel. 2015. "Study confirms that ending your texts with a period is terrible." The Washington Post. https://www.washingtonpost.com/news/speaking-of-science/wp/2015/12/08/study-confirms-that-ending-your-texts-with-a-period-is-terrible/

Chapter 3 – Meat of the Matter

Josephson, Brady. 2018. "The Advanced Guide to Integrated Fundraising." NextAfter Benchmark. https://www.nextafter.com/blog/advanced-guide-to-integrated-fundraising/

Dunhan, Trent. 2015. "The Imperative of Integrated Fundraising." The Giving Institute. https://www.givinginstitute.org/news/222095/The-Imperative-of-Integrated-Fundraising.htm

McPhillips, Christina and Offutt, Chas. 2018. "Social Media Paired with Email Yields 40 Percent More PBS Passport Revenue." PBS. https://pbs.app.box.com/s/awaz7ysjsj3mzeh2fzyp617ahns0rycf

Chapter 4 – Shake It Up

Lencioni, Patrick. 2004. Death by Meeting. Jossey-Bass a Wiley Imprint.

Chapter 5 – Ingredients for Project Success

Osterwalder, Alexander. 2010. Business Model Canvas Poster. Business Model Alchemist. http://www.businessmodelalchemist.com/tools

Chapter 6 – 86 the Turnover

Merhar, Christina. 2016. "Employee Retention: The Real Cost of Losing an Employee." PeopleKeep. Studies: Society for Human Resource Management (SHRM) and the Center for American Progress (CAP)
https://www.peoplekeep.com/blog/bid/312123/Employee-Retention-The-Real-Cost-of-Losing-an-Employee

Boushey, Heather and Glynn, Sarah Jane. 2012. "There are Significant Business Costs to Replacing Employees." Center for American Progress. https://www.americanprogress.org/wp-content/uploads/2012/11/CostofTurnover.pdf

Nonprofit HR and Guidestar. 2016. "Nonprofit Employment Practices SurveyTM Results." Nonprofit HR and Guidestar. https://www.nonprofithr.com/wp-content/uploads/2016/04/2016NEPSurvey-final.pdf

Grant, Corey C. 2017. "Why Nonprofits Must Pay More Attention to Burnout." CEO World Magazine. https://ceoworld.biz/2017/05/23/why-nonprofits-must-pay-more-attention-to-burnout/

Chapter 9 – The Regulars

McCaskill, Andrew. 2015. "Recommendations from Friends Remain Most Credible Form of Advertising." Nielsen.
https://www.nielsen.com/us/en/press-room/2015/recommendations-from-friends-remain-most-credible-form-of-advertising.html

Greenfieldboyce, Nell. 2012. "Web Cartoonist Raises 1 Million for Tesla Museum." NPR Morning Edition.
https://www.npr.org/2012/08/24/159925435/web-cartoonist-raises-1-million-for-tesla-museum

Inman, Matthew. 2013. "Why Nikola Tesla Was the Greatest Geek Who Ever Lived." The Oatmeal.
http://theoatmeal.com/comics/tesla

The Oatmeal. 2013. "Tesla Museum Saved." The Oatmeal.
http://theoatmeal.com/blog/tesla_museum_saved

Chapter 11 – Caviar

Sedghi, Amy. 2014. "Facebook: Ten Years of Social Networking, in Numbers."The Guardian.
https://www.theguardian.com/news/datablog/2014/feb/04/facebook-in-numbers-statistics

Ostrow, Adam. 2009. "Twitter's Massive 2008: 752 Percent Growth." Mashable Australia.
https://mashable.com/2009/01/09/twitter-growth-2008/#UWMQp8X56Gqh

LinkedIn. 2018. "About LinkedIn." LinkedIn Newsroom
https://ourstory.linkedin.com/

Chapter 12 – Happy Hour & Daily Specials

Association of Fundraising Professionals. 2018. "Fundraising Effectiveness Project." AFP
http://afpfep.org/reports/download/

Bloomerang, DonorPerfect, eTapestry and Neon. 2017. "2017 Fundraising Effectiveness Survey Results." Bloomerang.
https://bloomerang.co/blog/infographic-2016-fundraising-effectiveness-donor-retention-supplement

Made in the USA
Coppell, TX
07 February 2020